PENGUIN HANDBOOKS
PENGUIN LIVING CRAFTS
General Editor: Walter Brooks

AMERICAN FOLK TOYS

Dick Schnacke decided to make folk toys his specialty after helping to organize the Mountain State Arts and Craft Fair for the West Virginia Centennial, in 1963. He now owns and operates the Mountain Craft Shop in Proctor, West Virginia. The nation's leading producer of folk toys, the shop turns out more than a hundred thousand toys a year, all hand-made by some forty craftsmen-neighbors and all in demand by museums, stores, and individual buyers throughout the country.

AMERICAN folk toys

HOW TO MAKE THEM

Illustrated by the author

DICK SCHNACKE

Penguin Books Inc
Baltimore ● Maryland

To Jeanne, who always has helped in all my endeavors,
regardless of how unusual they may have seemed

Penguin Books Inc
7110 Ambassador Road
Baltimore, Maryland 21207, U.S.A.

First published by G. P. Putnam's Sons, New York, 1973
Published by Penguin Books Inc, 1974

Printed in the United States of America

CONTENTS

ACKNOWLEDGMENTS

Much of the credit for the identification and preservation of many folk toys of earlier times must go to Richard Chase, author and folklore lecturer. He engaged in research of folktales, folk music, and folk toys in the mountain areas of North Carolina at various times between 1935 and 1964. Mr. Chase is semiretired and lives in California.

Additional credit certainly must go to Jack Guy, who acted as Mr. Chase's chauffeur in the North Carolina mountains. With local artisans there he has continued to develop and carry on an important cottage industry production of folk toys.

Without the help of numerous West Virginia craftsmen in reviving folk toys, this book probably would not have been attempted. I especially want to thank Pemperton Cecil, Pete and Alice Postlethwait, Bessie Nice, Myrtle Patterson, Jack Herrmann and their families for great contributions, cooperation and trust. There are many other craftsmen who have done almost as much.

Don Page and Tom Screven of the West Virginia Department of Commerce have given key assistance beyond the normal scope of their jobs.

Substantial credit must go to the many, many individuals who continue to make suggestions regarding toys they remember from the past. Some of these contributors I know well; others I do not know by name because of the casual contacts. All are interested in preserving and extending the knowledge of true American folk toys, and their efforts are appreciated.

PREFACE

The definition of "folk toy" would be similar to that of "folktale" or "folk song." Its origin is lost to history, but it was created by someone for his own use. It may have been changed a little from being handed down from one generation to another. Still, it has been appreciated by many people over a long period of time and has been in wide use at certain times. A folk toy may have been almost forgotten during the last generation or two, but recent increased interest in the early ways of living may be focusing new attention on it.

Such a definition of "folk toy" would include all previously popular toys handmade by people for their own use. It would not include factory-made toys, even though there have been many popular in their day, such as Raggedy Ann, Teddy Bear, Barbie doll, cast-iron toys and electric trains. These mostly have required industrial equipment to produce, not available to an individual, and most were protected by copyrights or patents.

Folk toys are fun! A study of their design and function will reveal that the people of past generations were extremely inventive and resourceful. They could take an idea and, at little or no material cost, could fabricate an effective toy for themselves. The fact that many toys were tricky attests to the sense of humor of the early maker and user.

Whether one wishes to study folk toys or to make a few for his own use, there is a great deal of unique enjoyment to be had in this area.

The retail value of modern toys sold in the United States is approaching $3 billion a year. Toys constitute a very sizable industry. Toys today are mass-produced in factories from plastics, steel, and paper. They are manufactured on automated molding machines, punch presses, and printing presses. They are handled on mechanical conveyors and packaged without being touched by hand. The subject matter of today's toys often is space exploration, custom automobiles, military hardware, or fantasy. The demand is created by television advertising, which often exaggerates the size or realism of the toys. Many toys seem to be built for planned obsolescence; many break after the first use. The prices are high, but kids today either have the money or can persuade their parents to purchase them. It wasn't always this way.

In earlier days, living was not so complicated, but it was harder. There was little money available, and certainly not much of it could be spent on toys. There were few stores that would even carry toys.

But the demand for toys existed, so the children and their parents used the only means available: They made their own. They were proud of their ingenious creations and they played with them. In few cases is it known who originated a design, but the designs were copied and improved and passed down to the present time.

Many old folk toys utilize principles of physics which may baffle people even today. Look at the flipperdinger, the whimmydiddle, and the skyhook, for example. You may be startled when you see them demonstrated.

People today, especially the young, are thinking about ecology, Mother Earth, and a return to the older and simpler ways. So when they see a folk toy with its simple ingenuity and its native materials, naturally they find it attractive. And older people have nostalgia for ways of the past. In the folk toy field the generation gap has been bridged, for these "naturalized" toys are spontaneous, forthright, and genuine.

Folk toys are best known today in the middle and southern Appalachian regions of the United States but even there only by a small minority. The toys were popular in these areas, possibly because of the isolation in early days and partly because the inhabitants were mechanically inventive by nature.

Although the folk toys portrayed in this book include the more important ones, undoubtedly the list is incomplete. You may remember others, in which case the author would like to hear about them.

You may be familiar with some of the toys shown but under different names. This was often the case, a result of a folk heritage being passed on by word of mouth. But in every case, the names were descriptive of the toy's function.

DICK SCHNACKE

Mountain Craft Shop
Route 1
Proctor, West Virginia 26055

ACTION AND SKILL TOYS

Flipperdinger

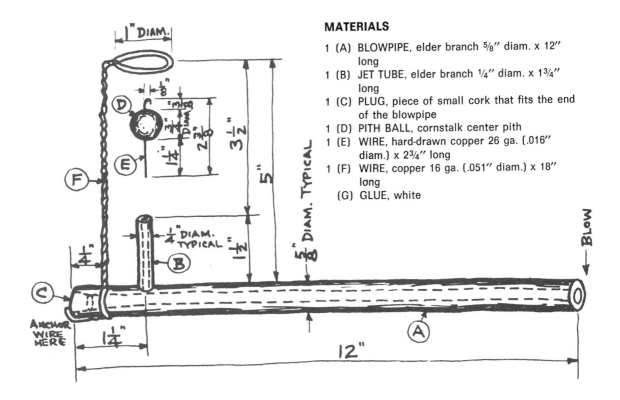

MATERIALS

1 (A) BLOWPIPE, elder branch ⅝" diam. x 12" long

1 (B) JET TUBE, elder branch ¼" diam. x 1¾" long

1 (C) PLUG, piece of small cork that fits the end of the blowpipe

1 (D) PITH BALL, cornstalk center pith

1 (E) WIRE, hard-drawn copper 26 ga. (.016" diam.) x 2¾" long

1 (F) WIRE, copper 16 ga. (.051" diam.) x 18" long

   (G) GLUE, white

This contrivance has a strong immediate appeal to all who see it for the first time. It looks like a miniature takeoff on the game of basketball but is several times older than basketball, which originated in 1891. A flipperdinger is a blowpipe with an air outlet on the top side. A hoop or ring of wire is fastened to the blowpipe and stands several inches above it. A ball has a very small wire with a hook on it pushed through its center.

When you blow on the blowpipe, the little ball resting on the air tube rises toward the hoop. It is a principle of physics that the ball will try to remain on the airstream instead of falling off. It keeps floating high while you attempt to hook the ball onto the hoop. If you're not successful, bend the hoop wire to a more favorable location (this is not considered cheating). After you've hooked the ball, blow again and try to get the ball unhooked and back into the starting hole. This is much more difficult but can occasionally be done.

Dry elder branches, sumac, or river cane may be used for the blowpipe stem and for the jet tube. Ream out the center pith from the blowpipe and jet tube, using a coat hanger wire or a 22-caliber rifle cleaning brush. Plug the end of the blowpipe by gluing in a piece of cork. Drill a hole for the jet tube and glue it in. Twist together the larger wire, forming the hoop and support; anchor it by bending the wire back against the cork.

Cut pith from the center of a dry cornstalk or other lightweight material; trim it to a rough ball shape. Sand and roll it in the palms of the hands to make a true spherically shaped pith ball. Form a hook on the small wire, insert the wire through the center of the pith ball, and glue it in place.

Whirligig

This toy is a first cousin to the flipperdinger. It uses the same type of blowpipe made of elder, sumac, or river cane. However, instead of blowing a pith ball upward, the airstream is directed tangentially to the blades of a paddle wheel rotor. Blowing on the pipe causes the rotor to turn. Small glass beads may be used as bearings for the wire rotor shaft.

The double whirligig has a single blowpipe with two air outlets directed tangentially at two paddle wheels. Blowing on the pipe causes both wheels to rotate at the same time but in opposite directions.

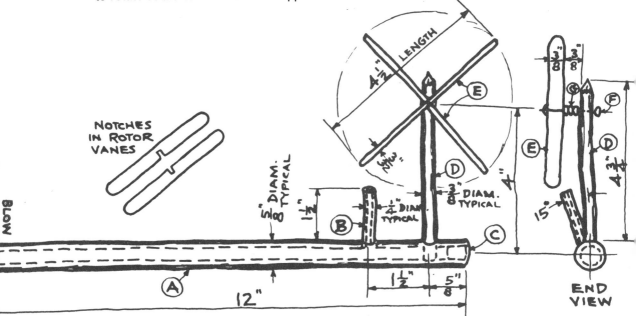

MATERIALS

1 (A) BLOWPIPE, elder branch 5/8″ diam. x 12″ long
1 (B) JET TUBE, elder branch 1/4″ diam. x 1 3/4″ long
1 (C) PLUG, piece of small cork that fits the end of the blowpipe
1 (D) UPRIGHT, wooden branch 3/8″ diam. x 5″ long
2 (E) ROTOR, wooden ice-cream bar sticks 3/32″ x 3/8″ x 4 1/2″
1 (F) AXLE, wire from a paper clip
5 (G) BEARINGS, small glass beads
  (H) GLUE, white

Dry elder branches, sumac, or river cane may be used for the blowpipe stem and jet tube, the same as on the flipperdinger. Ream out the center pith with a coathanger wire or with a 22-caliber rifle cleaning brush. Plug the end by gluing in a piece of cork. Drill a hole for the jet tube and glue it in. Drill a hole for the upright wooden branch, angled slightly away from the jet tube (about 15°), and glue it in. Drill a small hole for the rotor axle.

Notch the two wooden ice-cream bar sticks at their centers halfway through, and glue together in egg-crate-type construction to form the rotor. Straighten out a paper clip to make a wire axle. Wrap the wire around the center of the rotor to anchor it. Use the small glass beads for bearings and spacers on the axle. One bead should be embedded in each side of the upright and glued in. The axle shaft should be able to turn freely and should be anchored by crimping or bending the wire at the outer end.

Double Whirligig

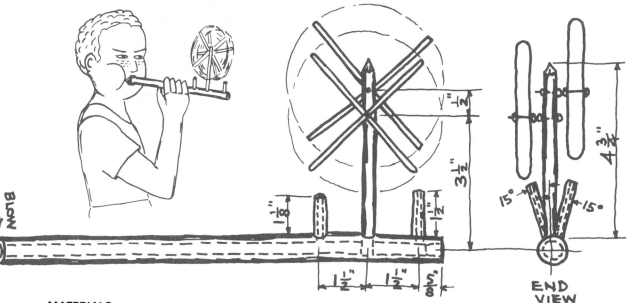

END VIEW

MATERIALS

Same as for single whirligig, except increase quantities to:

2 (B)
4 (E)
2 (F)
10 (G)

DOUBLE WHIRLIGIG

ALL DIMENSIONS NOT SHOWN ARE SAME AS FOR SINGLE WHIRLIGIG

The construction is the same as that of the single whirligig, except that two rotors and two jet tubes are used. The jet tubes are offset about 15° from the upright on both sides to cause the twin rotors to rotate in opposite directions when the blowpipe is blown.

Whimmydiddle

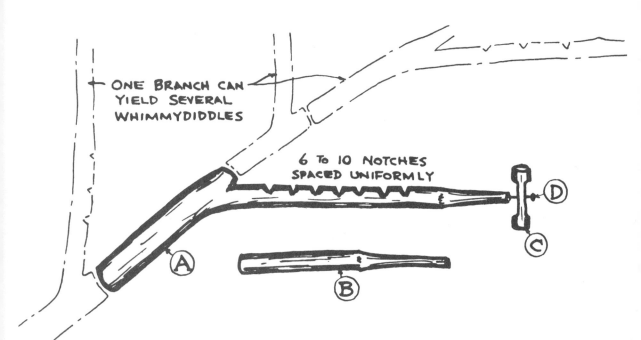

ONE BRANCH CAN YIELD SEVERAL WHIMMYDIDDLES

6 TO 10 NOTCHES SPACED UNIFORMLY

A

B

C

D

(HOOEY STICK OR GEE-HAW)

This stick seems to be magic. When another stick is rubbed across its notches, the little propeller at the end is caused to turn. When it is rubbed differently, the rotor turns in the opposite direction. These "gee" and "haw" movements have created a legend that the whimmydiddle is a lie detector, but actually the operator controls the "true" and "false" answers.

Nevertheless, the toy utilizes several principles of physics. As one account tells it: "The variably generated vibration frequencies and harmonics thereof react in concert upon the main body of given mass and configuration to set up vibration patterns and nodes which agitate the essentially statically balanced and frictionless rotor into rhythmic rotational movement. Naturally these factors vary from one piece of wood to another. Understand?"

Unusual variations of the whimmydiddle have been made. The double model has two rotors on the same shaft; other multiple shaft models have been made from a forked tree branch. One model had six rotors, all of which would turn simultaneously when the notched handle was rubbed.

16

MATERIALS

1 (A) BODY, hardwood branch, 7″ to 9″ long
1 (B) RUBBING STICK, hardwood branch, 4″ long
1 (C) ROTOR, hardwood twig, 3/16″ diam. x 1½″ long
1 (D) NAIL, box nail, 1″ long, small diam.

Use any small hardwood branch which does not have a pithy center. Green (live) wood is easiest to carve and will harden as it dries. Variations in size and shape can add interest. Cut the sticks shown. Carve down the end of the body and the end of the rubbing stick. Carve six to ten notches, about ⅛″ deep and evenly spaced, into the top edge of the body. Carve out the rotor to concentrate weight at its ends. Drill a hole in the center of the rotor for the nail. Drive the nail into the end of the body, leaving the rotor free to rotate. Test the whimmydiddle by rubbing the notches briskly, using the rubbing stick. If the rotor will not turn or reverse properly, keep carving down the diameter of the body and/or deepen the notches. When the whimmydiddle reaches the "happy spot," then stop carving.

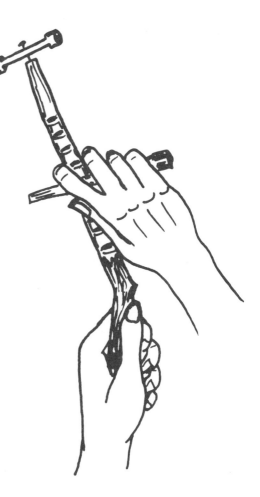

Buzz Saw

(BUTTON ON A STRING OR MOON WINDER)

A large button or other disk is threaded with a long double string through the buttonholes. The disk is started to wind up on the string by flipping. Then, by intermittent pulls on the ends of the string, the oscillating motion of the button increases in speed. At high speed it may sing like a circular saw blade.

In the old days, a boy at school would run a buzz saw into the pigtails of the girl sitting at the desk ahead of him, causing an awful snarl in her hair.

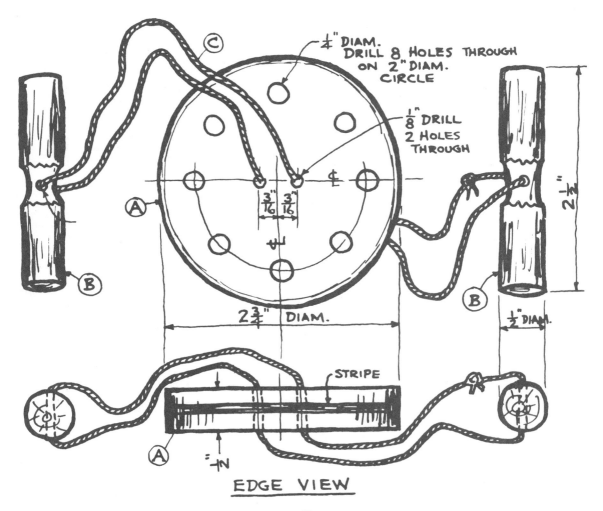

EDGE VIEW

MATERIALS

1 (A) DISK, hardwood 2¾″ diam. x ½″ long
2 (B) HANDLES, wooden branches ½″ diam. x
      2½″ long
1 (C) CORD, #21 nylon, 185 lb. test, 40″ long
   (D) PAINT, colored enamel

IN USE

The buzz saw can be made from nothing more than a large button and a piece of string. However, it is more fun to make a much larger one from a piece of wood. The disk may be sawed from a flat board, but a better-balanced buzz saw can be made by turning it from a solid piece of wood in a lathe. Choose wood with uniform grain so that the buzz saw will not be out of balance. While the disk is still in the lathe, the lathe may be slowed down to its slowest speed to paint a colored stripe around the rim. When a small paint brush is applied to the rotating disk it instantly makes a small stripe around the rim. Holes are drilled uniformly through the rim to make the disk sing a little as it runs. The two center holes are for the string and must be carefully centered on the disk so that it will be balanced.

Handles are recommended for the larger buzz saw so that your fingers won't get pinched. The cord is threaded through the disk and through the two handles, then tied securely so that the knot will not become untied under high-running stresses.

Ball and Cup

(OR CUP AND BALL)

This tester of dexterity has been popular in many cultures throughout the world and has taken various forms. It consists of a wooden cup on a handle and a small wooden ball fastened by a cord to the handle. The object is to swing the ball up and to land it in the cup. How many can you get in ten tries?

The handle may be on the axis of the cup and directly below it; in fact, it all may be one piece of wood. Or the handle may be at right angles to the axis of the cup, making the assembly resemble a giant smoking pipe.

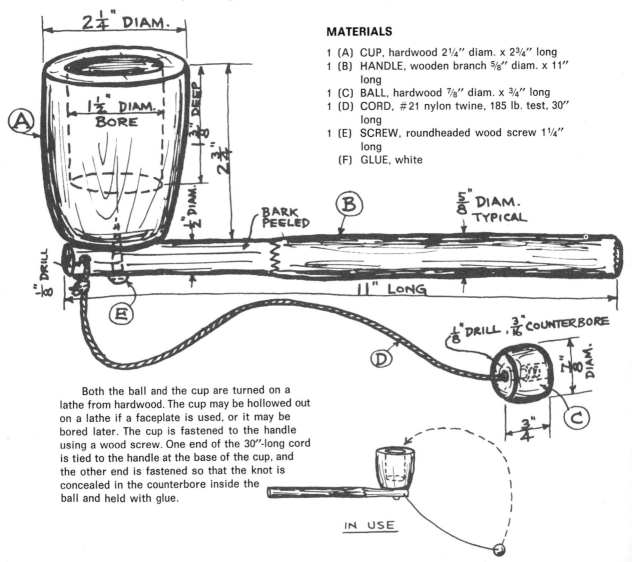

MATERIALS

1 (A) CUP, hardwood 2¼″ diam. x 2¾″ long
1 (B) HANDLE, wooden branch ⅝″ diam. x 11″ long
1 (C) BALL, hardwood ⅞″ diam. x ¾″ long
1 (D) CORD, #21 nylon twine, 185 lb. test, 30″ long
1 (E) SCREW, roundheaded wood screw 1¼″ long
  (F) GLUE, white

Both the ball and the cup are turned on a lathe from hardwood. The cup may be hollowed out on a lathe if a faceplate is used, or it may be bored later. The cup is fastened to the handle using a wood screw. One end of the 30″-long cord is tied to the handle at the base of the cup, and the other end is fastened so that the knot is concealed in the counterbore inside the ball and held with glue.

IN USE

Hoop Roll

Simple though it sounds, it can be fascinating just to run along rolling a hoop or a wheel, using a stick for a pusher. In earlier times many kids did this. With a little practice you could learn to steer around a twisting path.

The hoop usually was from a discarded keg or barrel, or sometimes a wheel from a toy wagon or doll carriage was used. The stick often was a piece of wooden lath; sometimes a second T-shaped piece was nailed on for easier operation.

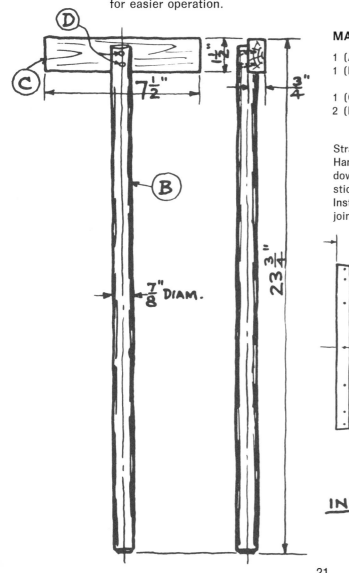

MATERIALS

1 (A) HOOP, steel band from end of nail keg
1 (B) STICK, wooden tree branch, 7/8″ diam. x 23½″ long
1 (C) T BAR, wood 7½″ x 1½″ x 3/4″
2 (D) SCREWS, 1″ long flathead wood screws

Locate a suitable hoop, band or wheel. Straighten it, making it as round as possible. Hammer out any nail holes in the hoop, and file down any sharp edges. Cut out the T bar and the stick, then notch and drill for the screw holes. Install the two screws, which will give a better joint than nails, although nails may be used.

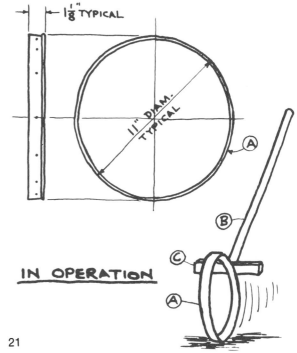

IN OPERATION

Jacob's Ladder

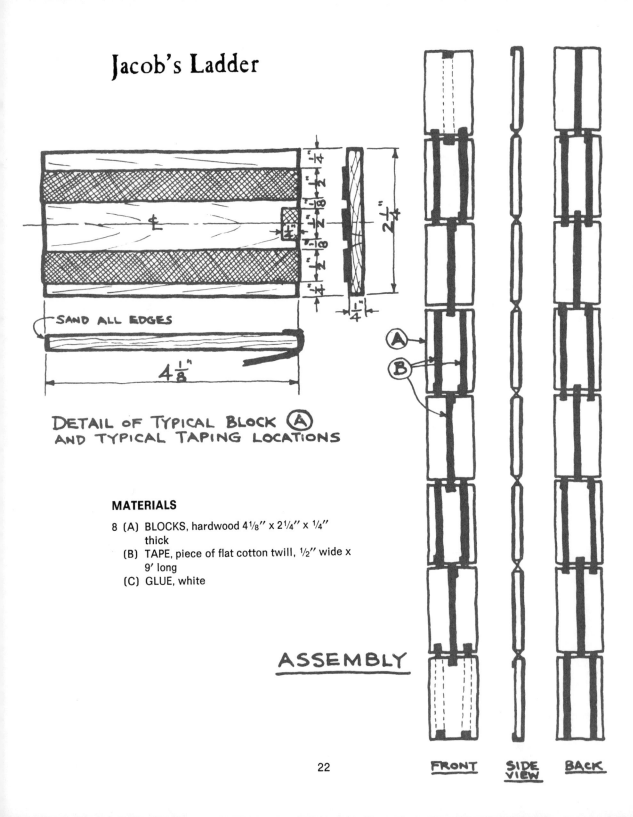

SAND ALL EDGES

$4\frac{1}{8}''$

DETAIL OF TYPICAL BLOCK (A) AND TYPICAL TAPING LOCATIONS

$2\frac{1}{4}''$

$\frac{1}{4}''$

MATERIALS

8 (A) BLOCKS, hardwood $4\frac{1}{8}'' \times 2\frac{1}{4}'' \times \frac{1}{4}''$ thick
  (B) TAPE, piece of flat cotton twill, $\frac{1}{2}''$ wide x 9' long
  (C) GLUE, white

(A)
(B)

ASSEMBLY

FRONT   SIDE VIEW   BACK

This toy has immediate appeal because it is both spectacular and mystifying. A series of flat wooden blocks, usually five to eight, are linked together by glued cloth tapes in such a way that they hinge against each other and create an illusion of tumbling down. The endmost block is grasped by its edges and tipped to touch the second block, which triggers the tumbling action, then tipped back to touch the second block again. This may be repeated indefinitely, sending ripples down the ladder.

The Jacob's ladder after which the toy is named is mentioned in the Bible, Genesis 28:12. Millions of these toys were imported to America from Japan in the early 1900's.

A dollar bill may be folded into quarters and placed behind the tape of one of the blocks. When the ladder is operated, the dollar suddenly will disappear and then reappear. As suspected, it moves to the back side; but in doing so, note that it actually transfers from behind a block with single tapes to a block with *double* tapes quicker than the eye can detect it!

Cut the eight blocks to size; make all edges smooth by sanding.

Lay the blocks end to end on a table. Follow the assembly diagram in gluing the tapes to the blocks, cutting each piece of tape to the length of the connection required. Apply glue only to the tape at the end of the block and to the 1/4" of overlap at the end of the tape so that the remainder of the tape is free to hinge and move. Keep the assembly of tapes as tightly together as possible. Allow the glue to dry completely before testing.

If the assembly of the tapes has been done correctly, each joint will serve as a double-acting hinge. When the Jacob's ladder is held by an end block and tipped back and forth, the blocks appear to be tumbling downward continuously.

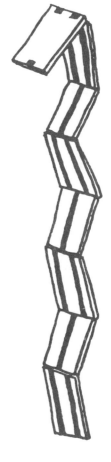

IN USE

FOLDED

23

Do-Nothing Machine

(OR SMOKE GRINDER)

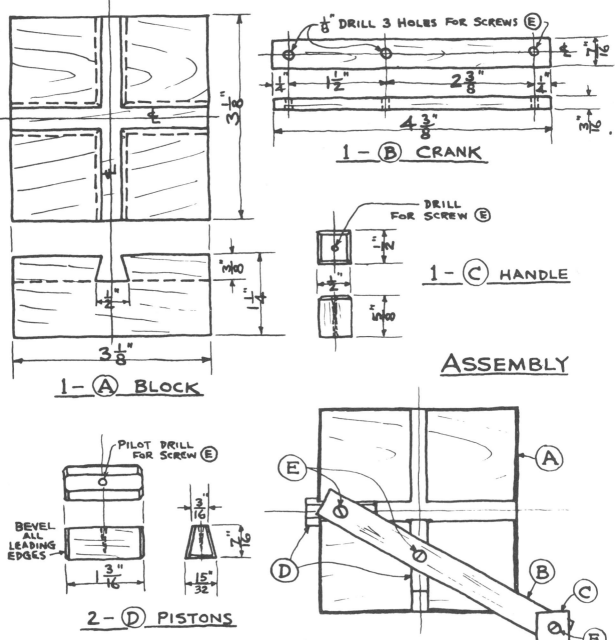

$\frac{1}{8}$" DRILL 3 HOLES FOR SCREWS Ⓔ

$\frac{7}{16}$"

$\frac{1}{4}$" | $1\frac{1}{2}$" | $2\frac{3}{8}$" | $\frac{1}{4}$"

$4\frac{3}{8}$"

$\frac{3}{16}$"

1 – Ⓑ CRANK

DRILL FOR SCREW Ⓔ

$\frac{1}{2}$"

$\frac{3}{8}$"

1 – Ⓐ BLOCK

$3\frac{1}{8}$"

$\frac{3}{8}$"

$\frac{1}{4}$"

$\frac{1}{2}$"

1 – Ⓒ HANDLE

PILOT DRILL FOR SCREW Ⓔ

BEVEL ALL LEADING EDGES

$1\frac{3}{16}$"

$\frac{3}{16}$"

$\frac{7}{16}$"

$\frac{15}{32}$"

2 – Ⓓ PISTONS

ASSEMBLY

Ⓐ Ⓔ Ⓓ Ⓑ Ⓒ Ⓔ

This device does only what its name implies, but it does a good job of that! It is a block of wood with two dovetail grooves milled into it at right angles to each other. In each groove is a little wooden piston, and the two pistons are connected by a crank arm. When the crank handle is turned, the pistons move back and forth across the block but never strike each other. The handle can be turned around and around, accomplishing nothing except creating laughter.

Surprisingly, the handle does not follow a circular path as it is turned, but rather it describes the shape of an ellipse, or oval. So actually the do-nothing machine does do something! In the science of machine kinematics, it is known as an elliptical trammel and is used in drawing ellipses. A similar mechanism called the elliptical chuck has been used in machining elliptical sections.

Sometimes called a smoke grinder, this toy can be confused with another smoke grinder which is a toy version of a primitive drill.

MATERIALS

1 (A) BLOCK, hardwood 3⅛" x 3⅛" x 1¼"
1 (B) CRANK, hardwood 4⅜" x 7/16" x 3/16"
1 (C) HANDLE, hardwood ⅝" x ½" x ½"
2 (D) PISTONS, hardwood 1 3/16" x 15/32" x 7/16"
3 (E) WOOD SCREWS, roundheaded ½" long
  (F) GLUE, white

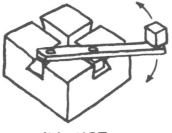

IN USE

Cut out the various parts, using contrasting wood colors, if possible, for better appearance.

Cut the two intersecting dovetail grooves into the block, using a router with a ½"-wide dovetail cutter going ⅜" deep. To prevent the block from chipping when the cutter enters or leaves the cut, it is advisable to clamp the block between two scrap blocks while cutting.

Drill the three holes in the crank and the pilot holes in the handle and pistons for screws. Bevel all leading edges of the pistons to prevent them from binding in the grooves. When the final assembly fitting is done, the screws may be glued in so that they will not loosen from use. A little paraffin wax applied to the grooves will smooth the operation.

At first glance, one would think that the cutting of the dovetail grooves is the most difficult part of making this device. Actually, the shaping and proper fitting of the pistons are much more difficult.

Operating this toy requires no talent whatsoever. Just crank it!

Stick Horse

It takes a lot of imagination to believe you are riding a horse when you are actually walking or running, but small children are very capable of this. The stick horse has a horse's head and a bridle, but the rest of it is only a stick straddled by the rider and dragging on the ground.

The stick horse may be very simple and crude, or it may be finely detailed, including painted or carved features, ears, mane, bit and leather bridle, a tail, and even a wheel on the end of the stick.

MATERIALS

1 (A) STICK, wooden branch 1″ diam. x 30″ long
1 (B) HEAD, wood ¾″ x 7¼″ x 9″
1 (C) HANDLEBAR, wooden branch ⅝″ diam. x 8″ long
1 (D) PIN, birch dowel ½″ diam. x 3″ long
1 (E) BRIDLE, leather ½″ wide, approx. 32″ long
1 (F) REINS, leather ½″ wide, approx. 38″ long
1 (G) MANE, sheepskin
2 (H) EARS, leather 2½″ x 3″
   (I) TACKS, ornamental brass upholstery tacks
   (J) GLUE, white
   (K) PAINT, black and red

ASSEMBLY

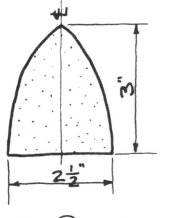

2 — (H) EARS
LEATHER

Cut out and sand the head; drill the hole for the handlebar and the hole for the dowel. Paint in the eye, nose, and mouth detail on both sides of the head. Cut natural wooden branches for the main stick and for the handlebar, chamfer ends and drill a hole for the dowel, and install them using glue. Cut out the mane and glue on. Cut leather pieces for the ears and fasten on either side by doubling the leather to make it stand up, then gluing and tacking. Cut strips of leather to make the bridle and reins, fastening with ornamental brass tacks for appearance.

The stick horse is ready for riding. The stick's length can be varied to fit the size of the child.

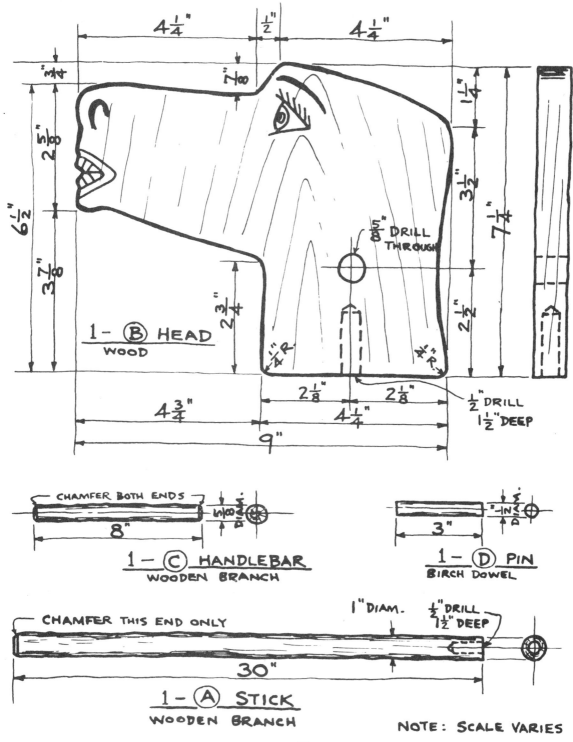

$4\frac{1}{4}"$ $\frac{1}{2}"$ $4\frac{1}{4}"$

$\frac{3}{4}"$

$\frac{1}{100}"$

$2\frac{5}{100}"$

$6\frac{1}{2}"$

$3\frac{7}{100}"$

$2\frac{3}{4}"$

$\frac{1}{4}R$

$\frac{1}{4}R$

$1\frac{1}{4}"$

$3\frac{1}{2}"$

$7\frac{1}{4}"$

$2\frac{1}{2}"$

$\frac{5}{8}"$ DRILL THROUGH

$\frac{1}{2}"$ DRILL $1\frac{1}{2}"$ DEEP

1— Ⓑ HEAD
WOOD

$4\frac{3}{4}"$

$2\frac{1}{8}"$ $2\frac{1}{8}"$

$4\frac{1}{4}"$

$9"$

CHAMFER BOTH ENDS $\frac{5}{100}"$ DIA.

$8"$

1— Ⓒ HANDLEBAR
WOODEN BRANCH

$\frac{3}{4}"$ DIA.

$3"$

1— Ⓓ PIN
BIRCH DOWEL

CHAMFER THIS END ONLY

$1"$ DIAM.

$\frac{1}{2}"$ DRILL $1\frac{1}{2}"$ DEEP

$30"$

1— Ⓐ STICK
WOODEN BRANCH

NOTE: SCALE VARIES

27

Smoke Grinder

This one is not to be confused with the do-nothing machine, which also is sometimes known as a smoke grinder. The toy actually is a small version of a primitive drill, which is still used by Indians of the American Southwest to drill holes through gemstones. They can actually wear a hole through a hard stone with a wooden stick when sand is used as an abrasive cutting compound.

The toy has a pointed wooden spindle with a wooden disk to store flywheel energy. A wooden handle fits loosely on the spindle and is connected by two short cords to the top of the spindle. When the spindle point is placed in a depression and the handle moved rapidly up and down, the cords wrap one way and then the other and cause the spindle to turn back and forth. The flywheel energy helps keep it in operation.

MATERIALS

1 (A) SPINDLE, birch dowel 1/4" diam. x 9" long
1 (B) YOKE, wood 4" x 3/4" x 1/2"
1 (C) FLYWHEEL, hardwood 2 1/2" diam. x 3/4" thick
1 (D) CORD, #21 nylon twine, 18" long
1 (E) BASE, wood 1 3/4" x 1 3/4" x 3/4"
  (F) GLUE, white

Cut the spindle to length, sharpen one end with a pencil sharpener, and saw a notch in the other end. Cut the yoke to size, drill the center hole, notch the two ends, and carve the depressions for finger grips. Make the flywheel perfectly round and balanced by drilling a hole and cutting out the disk using a 2 1/2" hole saw. Cut the base to size, center-punch it, and round and smooth all edges. Glue the flywheel onto the spindle. Tie knots in the ends of the cord and assemble. Adjust the length of the cord so that the spindle is about 1/2" above the flywheel when the cords are not twisted. Glue the cord into the spindle and the yoke.

To work the smoke grinder, place the base on a table; put the point of the spindle into the punched hole in the base. Wind the spindle up several turns. Grasp the spindle and, releasing the flywheel, work the spindle up and down repeatedly. This will wind and rewind the spindle, keeping it in operation.

ASSEMBLY

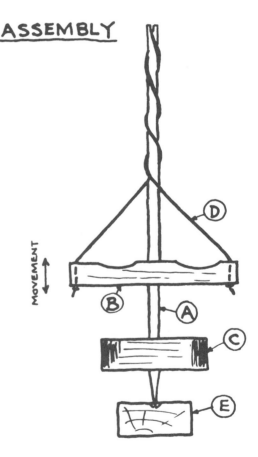

MOVEMENT

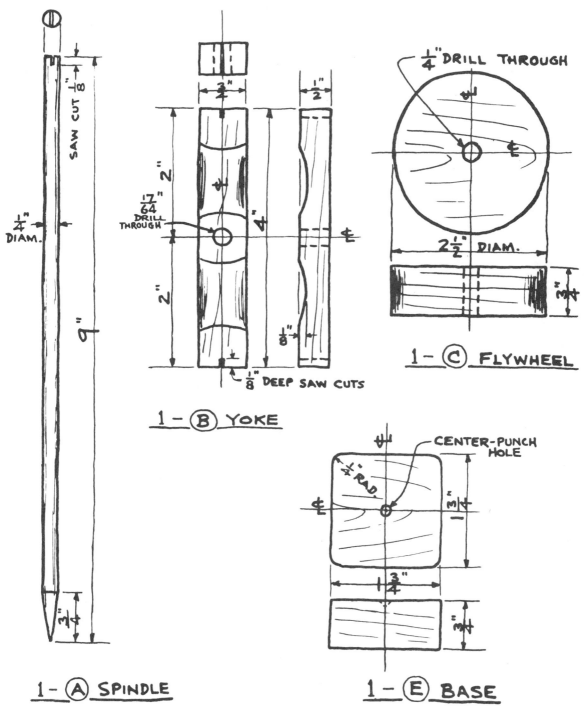

SAW CUT $\frac{1}{8}$"

$\frac{1}{4}$" DIAM.

9"

$\frac{3}{4}$"

1 – Ⓐ SPINDLE

$\frac{3}{2}$"

2"

$\frac{17}{64}$" DRILL THROUGH

2"

4"

$\frac{1}{2}$"

$\frac{1}{8}$"

$\frac{1}{8}$" DEEP SAW CUTS

1 – Ⓑ YOKE

$\frac{1}{4}$" DRILL THROUGH

$\frac{3}{4}$"

$2\frac{1}{2}$" DIAM.

$\frac{3}{4}$"

1 – Ⓒ FLYWHEEL

CENTER-PUNCH HOLE

$\frac{3}{4}$"

$\frac{1}{4}$" RAD.

$\frac{3}{4}$"

$\frac{3}{4}$"

$\frac{3}{4}$"

1 – Ⓔ BASE

Mountain Bolo

(OR ESKIMO YO-YO)

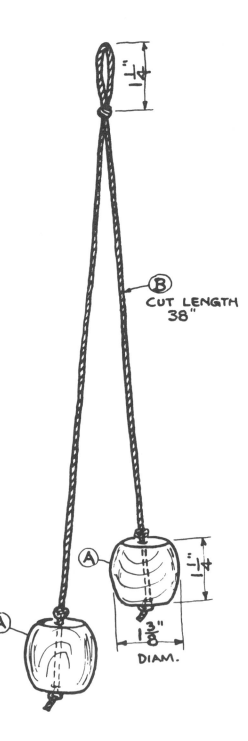

CUT LENGTH 38"

MATERIALS

2 (A) BALLS, hardwood 1⅜" diam. x 1¼" long
1 (B) CORD, #21 nylon twine, 185 lb. test, 38" long

The two balls are turned in a lathe and are drilled through their axes with a ⅛" drill. The cord is cut to 38", threaded through the two balls, and tied with an overhand knot on either side of the balls. The cord is tied with an overhand loop for a handhold. This loop is *near* the center, but one cord is slightly longer than the other. This lets the two balls pass each other without hitting.

This toy requires a little practice before it can be mastered. An easy way to begin is to place the bolo on the ground with the two balls out straight, and then pick up the loop in a straight-up movement. This gets you off to a good even start. Other methods of starting can be learned later.

1⅜" DIAM.

This skill toy consists of two small balls at the ends of a string. The string has a small loop near the center, but the lengths of string are unequal to avoid a clash of the weights. Grasping the center loop, the object is to make the two weights orbit in opposite directions (counterrotate) by moving the hand up and down or back and forth. This looks quite easy, but it isn't until the straight line movement is mastered.

The weights often are nuts (such as buckeyes and even machine nuts), while in the Eskimo yo-yo version of the polar regions small sealskin balls are filled with sand for weight. Although there is a resemblance, this toy is not to be confused with the recent clackers or click-clacks, which had two heavy plastic balls on equal lengths of string, allowing the balls to bounce back and forth with a similar movement. The mountain bolo probably inspired the plastic clackers, which have already been withdrawn from the market for safety reasons.

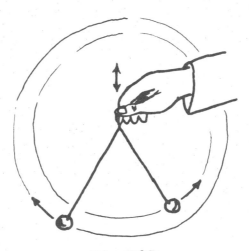

IN USE

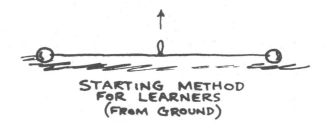

STARTING METHOD
FOR LEARNERS
(FROM GROUND)

Climbing Bear

Pull on one cord, then on the other. The geometry of the bear is such that at each pull it raises itself another step up the cords. When it arrives at the top, let go of the cords and it will slide down to the bottom, ready for another climb.

MATERIALS

1 (A) BODY, hardwood 5¾" x 2" x ⅜"
1 (B) BAR, wood 6¾" x ¾" x ⅜"
3 (C) BEADS, birch dowel ⅝" diam. x ⅝" long
4 (D) EYES, box nails ⅝" long
2 (E) NOSE, red thumbtacks
   (F) PEN, felt tip, black
1 (G) CORD, hard-braided cotton 5/32" diam.
         x 9'

Lay out and cut out all wooden parts. Drill the holes through the bear's paws, through the bar, and through the beads. Add the face decoration to both sides of the bear, consisting of nails for eyes, a red thumbtack for the nose and black pen lines for outline of the eyes and for the mouth.

Cut two lengths of cord each 50" long and thread through bar, bear, and beads as shown, knotting the ends. Use the remaining cord as the center support, passing it through the bar and the bead.

To make the bear climb, place the center support loop over a hook in the wall or the ceiling and pull alternately on the two cords. When the bear reaches the top, release both cords and it will slide back down.

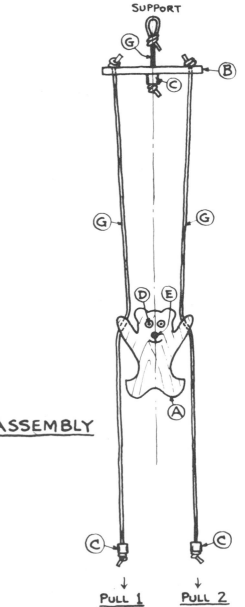

SUPPORT

ASSEMBLY

PULL 1   PULL 2

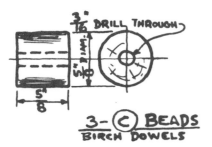

3"
16 DRILL THROUGH

⅝"
8

3- Ⓒ BEADS
BIRCH DOWELS

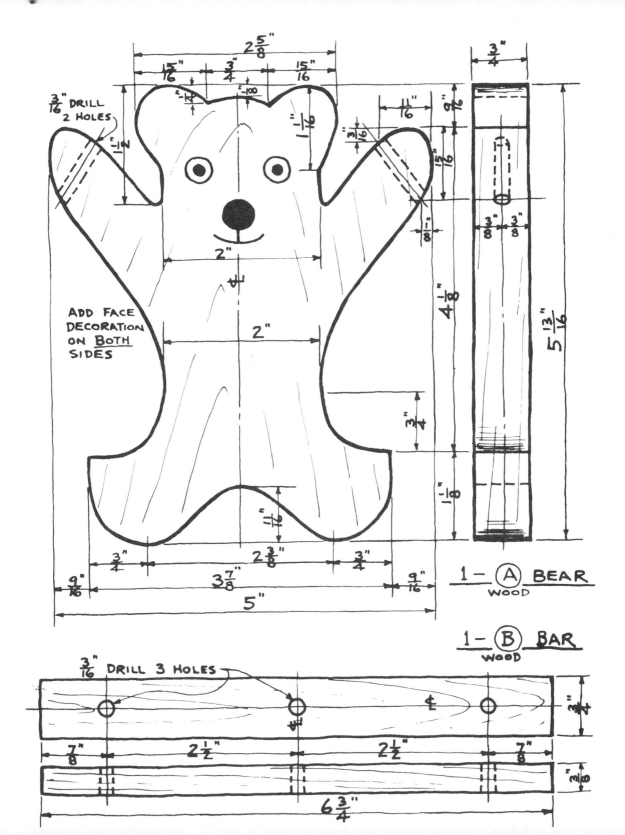

$2\frac{5}{8}"$

$\frac{15}{16}"$ $\frac{3}{4}"$ $\frac{15}{16}"$

$\frac{3}{16}"$ DRILL
2 HOLES

$1\frac{1}{2}"$

$\frac{11}{16}"$

$\frac{3}{16}"$

$\frac{9}{16}"$

$\frac{15}{16}"$

$\frac{1}{8}"$

$4\frac{1}{8}"$

$5\frac{13}{16}"$

$\frac{3}{4}"$

$\frac{3}{8}"$ $\frac{3}{8}"$

ADD FACE
DECORATION
ON BOTH
SIDES

2"

2"

$\frac{3}{4}"$

$1\frac{1}{8}"$

$\frac{1}{16}"$

$\frac{3}{4}"$ $2\frac{3}{8}"$ $\frac{3}{4}"$

$\frac{9}{16}"$ $3\frac{7}{8}"$ $\frac{9}{16}"$

5"

<u>1 — Ⓐ BEAR</u>
WOOD

<u>1 — Ⓑ BAR</u>
WOOD

$\frac{3}{16}"$ DRILL 3 HOLES

$\frac{3}{4}"$

$\frac{7}{8}"$ $2\frac{1}{2}"$ $2\frac{1}{2}"$ $\frac{7}{8}"$

$\frac{3}{16}"$

$6\frac{3}{4}"$

Finger Top

(OR WHIRLY TOP)

MATERIAL

1 (A) TOP, hardwood 1¾″ diam. x 1-13/16″ long

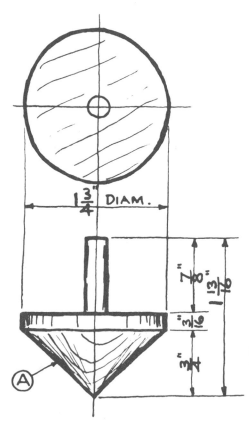

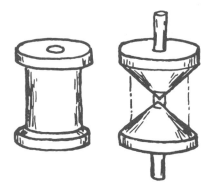

IF HAND-CARVED FROM A
THREAD SPOOL, FIT A
DOWEL INTO THE CENTER
HOLE. THE SPOOL CAN
MAKE 2 TOPS.

1¾″ DIAM.

SHOWN AS A
WOOD-TURNING

TOPS

This simple little top is spun with the fingers, but it will spin for a long time. It may be carved from a wooden spool with a dowel inserted as its spindle, or it may be completely turned on a lathe.

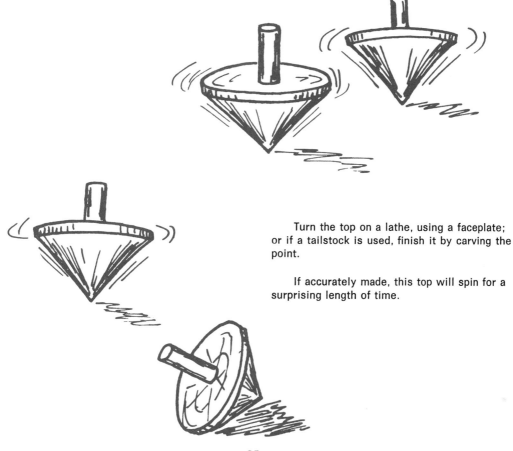

Turn the top on a lathe, using a faceplate; or if a tailstock is used, finish it by carving the point.

If accurately made, this top will spin for a surprising length of time.

Spinning Top

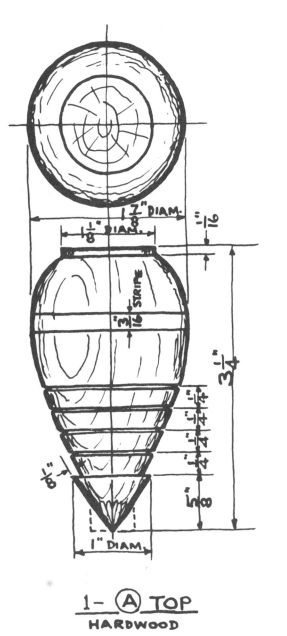

MATERIALS

1 (A) TOP, hardwood 2″ x 2″ x 5″ long
1 (B) STRING, hard-finished cotton 1/16″ diam.
     x 45″ long
  (C) PAINT, colored enamel

1 — Ⓐ TOP
HARDWOOD

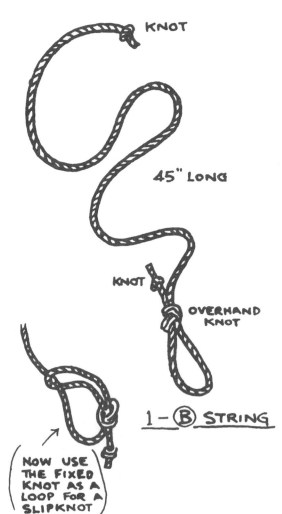

KNOT

45″ LONG

KNOT

OVERHAND
KNOT

1 — Ⓑ STRING

NOW USE
THE FIXED
KNOT AS A
LOOP FOR A
SLIPKNOT

This is a cone-shaped lathe-turned toy, which is caused to spin by wrapping a string around it and casting the top toward the ground. This top is difficult to spin, but in the hands of a child it can be done almost every time after some experimentation.

The top often has a steel spike in its end to avoid wear and to make it spin longer. A group of children spinning their tops may take turns trying intentionally to spike or split the other children's tops while they are spinning.

Traditionally, the top has a colorful striped line at the point of greatest diameter, which is applied while the top is still in the lathe.

This top is turned on a lathe between centers, including the processes of shaping, grooving and sanding, and then after removal from the machine the point is carved by hand with a knife. Leave about ½" diameter stock at the point for this purpose. There is no metal spike on this top, so it is not as likely to damage floors.

The purpose of the grooves around the top is to keep the string from sliding off. Before removing the top from the lathe, slow the machine down and apply the traditional stripe by touching a small paintbrush to the point of greatest diameter.

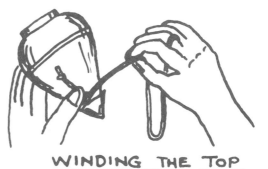

WINDING THE TOP

Tie a knot in each end of the string to prevent it from fraying. Tie another overhand knot to form a loop in the string. Then the fixed knot can act as a loop for a slipknot to go over the finger.

To spin the top, make a slipknot of the loop end of the string, and slip it over the middle finger of the right hand. Hold the top in the left hand, start the knotted end as shown, binding it and wrapping the string tightly with clockwise motion of the right hand until the string is entirely wrapped. Transfer the top to the right hand.

READY TO CAST

Now throw the top down onto the floor, pulling back your hand to give a whipping motion to the top and causing it to spin. Some repeated trials with varied angles of handholds will be needed before spinning can be mastered. Try all angles of holding, even with the top upside down.

Spindle Top

(OR MOUNTAIN TOP)

This top is spun with a cord or a shoelace and is similar to the spinning top. However, it has a framework to guide the top, and when the cord has been pulled away to start the spinning, the top will fall to the floor and spin. This type is very easy to spin.

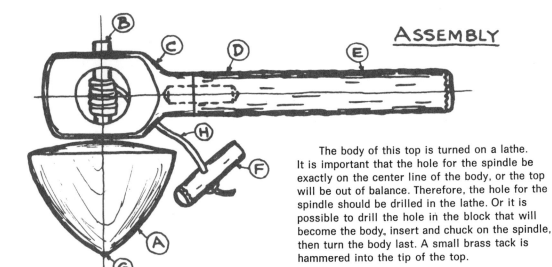

ASSEMBLY

The body of this top is turned on a lathe. It is important that the hole for the spindle be exactly on the center line of the body, or the top will be out of balance. Therefore, the hole for the spindle should be drilled in the lathe. Or it is possible to drill the hole in the block that will become the body, insert and chuck on the spindle, then turn the body last. A small brass tack is hammered into the tip of the top.

The yoke is shown as part of a lathe turning also, but it does not have to be turned as long as it has the drilled holes shown.

The handle is a natural branch of wood. The dowel and the spindle are the same size, 5/16" diameter. The ends of the handle, spindle and tab are chamfered for smooth handling. A hole is made in the spindle to insert the cord, which is a shoelace with a wooden tab on the end. Glue the spindle into the body, and the dowel into the yoke and the handle.

To spin the top, insert the spindle into the yoke. Put the tip of the shoelace into the hole in the spindle and wind it up by rotating the body. Now pull on the tab, and the top will drop out of the yoke, spinning.

MATERIALS

1 (A) BODY, hardwood 2¾" diam. x 2" long
1 (B) SPINDLE, birch dowel 5/16" diam. x 2½" long
1 (C) YOKE, hardwood 2¾" x 1½" x ¾"
1 (D) DOWEL, birch dowel 5/16" diam. x 1¼" long
1 (E) HANDLE, hardwood branch ¾" diam. x 4¾" long
1 (F) TAB, hardwood branch ⅜" diam. x 2" long
1 (G) TACK, roundheaded brass tack ⅛" diam.
1 (H) CORD, standard brown shoelace, 18" long
  (I) GLUE, white

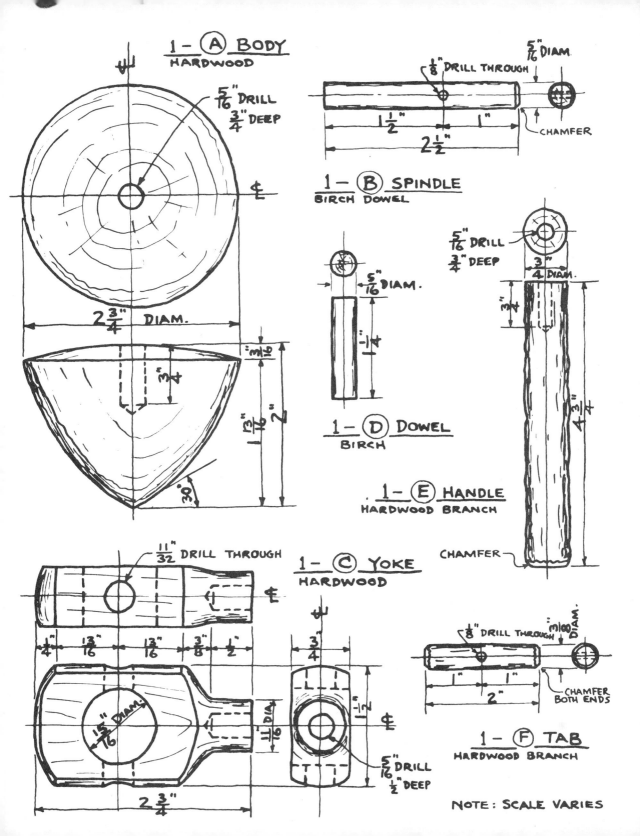

The Wrestlers

(OR DANCERS)

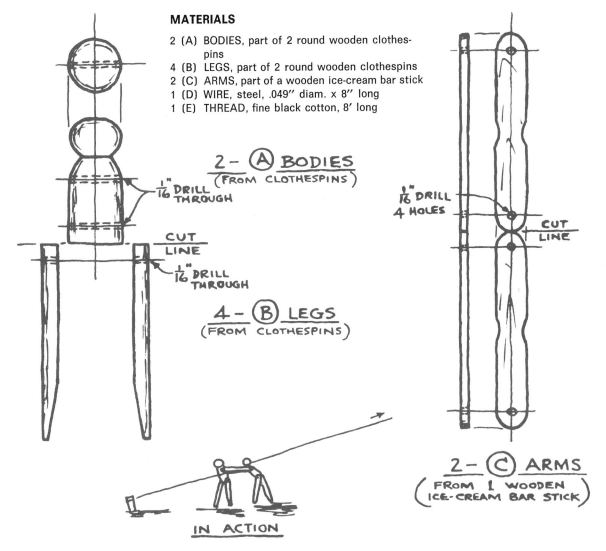

MATERIALS

- 2 (A) BODIES, part of 2 round wooden clothes-pins
- 4 (B) LEGS, part of 2 round wooden clothespins
- 2 (C) ARMS, part of a wooden ice-cream bar stick
- 1 (D) WIRE, steel, .049" diam. x 8" long
- 1 (E) THREAD, fine black cotton, 8' long

2 - Ⓐ BODIES
(FROM CLOTHESPINS)

$\frac{1}{16}$" DRILL THROUGH

CUT LINE

$\frac{1}{16}$" DRILL THROUGH

4 - Ⓑ LEGS
(FROM CLOTHESPINS)

$\frac{1}{16}$" DRILL 4 HOLES

CUT LINE

2 - Ⓒ ARMS
(FROM 1 WOODEN ICE-CREAM BAR STICK)

IN ACTION

40

ANIMATED TOYS

The two little wrestlers are very realistic, and the thread that causes their movement is almost invisible, which adds to the reality. The wrestlers are made from two wooden clothespins and a wooden ice-cream bar stick. The wrestlers usually are not painted; however, by decorating one as a man and one as a woman, they have been called the dancers.

No exact dimensions are given for the parts because of variations in the size of clothespins and ice-cream bar sticks. However the diagram may be used as a guide to scale.

Cut two clothespins as shown and drill the parts. Cut the ice-cream bar stick in the center, round the ends, and drill the holes. Use wire to make pins with loop heads for holding the arms and legs to the bodies. The assembly should be rather loose.

Tie a short piece of thread to one arm to act as a ground anchor when tied to a peg or a furniture leg. Tie a longer piece of thread to the other arm to be used for manipulating the wrestlers. This is done by jerking the thread lightly while the wrestlers are barely touching the ground. The black thread is almost invisible against most backgrounds.

ASSEMBLY

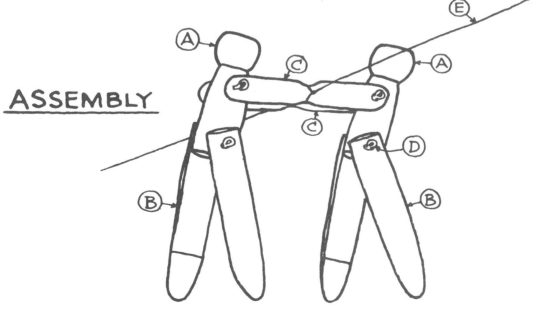

41

Limber Jack

(STOMPER DOLL OR DANCING MAN)

This toy is an articulated carved wooden figurine with legs and arms loosely fastened by pins. He is suspended by a hand stick in his back or in another version hanging from a cord. The operator sits on a thin overhanging board on a chair and taps the board with his hand. Touching the feet of the man to the vibrating board sets him into a rhythmic and realistic tap dance, tapping his feet and swinging his arms. The action seems most lifelike when performed to appropriate music, such as "Turkey in the Straw." The figure was usually made of unpainted wood except for the facial features. Some, however, were completely painted as black tap dancers.

The popularity of Limber Jack seems to have been inspired or at least promoted by the coming of the minstrel show and the showboats. The shows were rare entertainment for people of that more isolated time, and the vigorous tap dancers made a strong impression on them. Limber Jack, a toy having an identical action, was a reminder of the pleasant experience of viewing a show and hence became a popular folk toy.

MATERIALS

1 (A) BODY, hardwood 5¾″ x 2″ x ⅜″
2 (B) ARMS, hardwood 2 5/16″ x 1⅛″ x ⅜″
2 (C) UPPER LEGS, hardwood 2⅝″ x ½″ x ½″
2 (D) LOWER LEGS, hardwood 2⅝″ x ⅞″ x ⅜″
1 (E) STICK, hardwood branch with bark, ⅝″ diam. x 17″ long
1 (F) PADDLE, hardwood 23″ x 4″ x ¼″
1 (G) WIRE, steel .042″ gauge approx., 8″ long
  (H) PENS, felt tip, black and red, or PAINT

Cut the wood material for all items to rough size. Draw designs on all items as shown in the sketch. Saw all items to final shapes. Drill the required holes and hand-carve the rounded surfaces indicated on the body, legs and arms. Assemble joints loosely with pins made from straight lengths of the steel wire, bending over the ends to fasten the parts. Add facial features and buttons, as desired, using a pen or paintbrush. Sharpen the stick to a point to insert it firmly into the ¼″ hole in the back of the body.

Test the action of the dancer by sitting on the paddle on a chair, tapping the paddle with your free hand while touching Limber Jack's feet to the board.

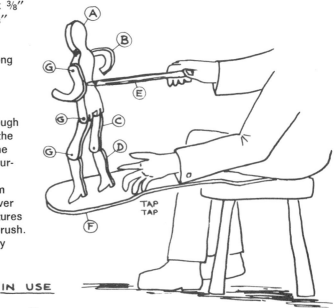

TAP
TAP

IN USE

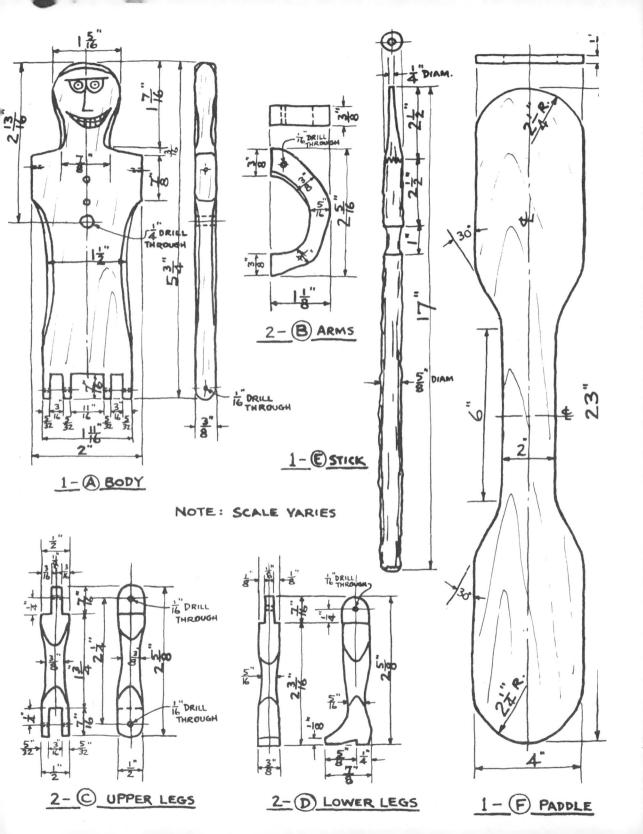

1 - Ⓐ BODY

2 - Ⓑ ARMS

1 - Ⓔ STICK

NOTE: SCALE VARIES

2 - Ⓒ UPPER LEGS

2 - Ⓓ LOWER LEGS

1 - Ⓕ PADDLE

Flap Jack
(THE ACROBAT)

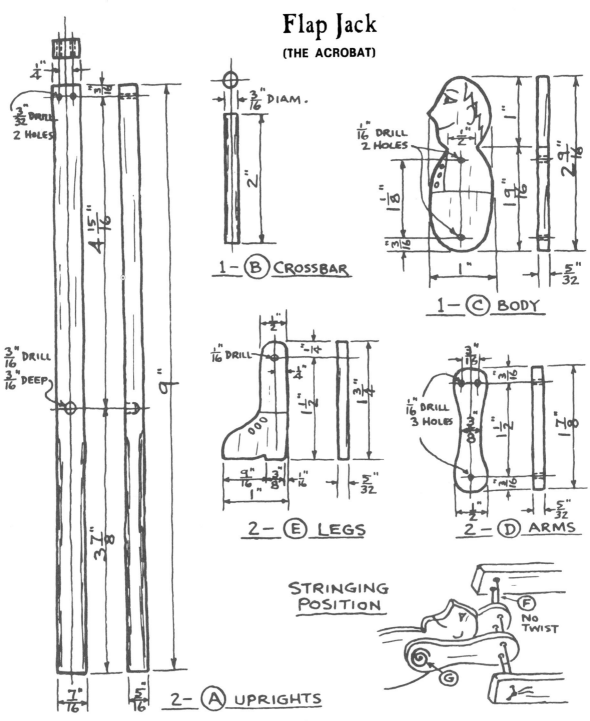

$\frac{1}{4}''$

$\frac{3}{14}''$

$\frac{3}{32}''$ DRILL
2 HOLES

$4\frac{15}{16}''$

$\frac{3}{16}''$ DRILL
$\frac{3}{16}''$ DEEP

$9''$

$3\frac{7}{8}''$

$\frac{7}{16}''$ $\frac{5}{16}''$

2 – Ⓐ UPRIGHTS

$\frac{3}{16}''$ DIAM.

$2''$

1 – Ⓑ CROSSBAR

$\frac{1}{16}''$ DRILL
2 HOLES

$\frac{1}{2}''$

$\frac{1}{8}''$

$\frac{3}{16}''$

$1''$

$1\frac{9}{16}''$

$2\frac{9}{16}''$

$\frac{5}{32}''$

1 – Ⓒ BODY

$\frac{1}{16}''$ DRILL

$\frac{1}{2}''$

$1\frac{1}{4}''$

$\frac{1}{4}''$

$1\frac{1}{2}''$

$3\frac{3}{4}''$

000

$\frac{9}{16}''$ $\frac{3}{8}''$ $\frac{1}{16}''$

$1''$

$\frac{5}{32}''$

2 – Ⓔ LEGS

$\frac{3}{16}''$

$\frac{3}{16}''$

$\frac{1}{16}''$ DRILL
3 HOLES

$\frac{3}{8}''$

$\frac{1}{2}''$

$\frac{3}{16}''$

$1\frac{1}{2}''$

$3\frac{7}{10}''$

$\frac{1}{2}''$

$\frac{5}{32}''$

2 – Ⓓ ARMS

STRINGING POSITION

Ⓕ NO TWIST

Ⓖ

Here is the acrobat par excellence! Squeeze the lower handles of the framework, and Flap Jack performs all sorts of difficult acrobatic feats while swinging on the bar. The bar actually is a pair of strings passing through his hands, which, when twisted and tensioned by the squeeze of the handles, causes the articulated performer to delight his audience with his feats of strength and agility.

MATERIALS

2 (A) UPRIGHTS, straight-grained hardwood (oak or hickory) 9″ x 7/16″ x 5/16″
1 (B) CROSSBAR, birch dowel 3/16″ diam. x 2″ long
1 (C) BODY, wood 2 9/16″ x 1″ x 5/32″
2 (D) ARMS, wood 1 7/8″ x 1/2″ x 5/32″
2 (E) LEGS, wood 1 3/4″ x 1″ x 5/32″
1 (F) STRING, braided nylon fishline, .010″ diam. x 20″ long
1 (G) WIRE, low-voltage hookup wire .040″ diam. x 8″ long
   (H) GLUE, white
   (I) PEN, fine felt tip, black

Lay out and cut out the various wooden parts required. Drill all holes shown, and round the uprights in the gripping area by carving with a knife. Glue the crossbar in place between the uprights. Round the edges of all parts of the body, arms and legs to give a hand-carved appearance. Use a fine felt-tip pen to add details to both sides of the body and legs.

Attach the arms to the body by threading a piece of wire through the proper holes and retaining it by making a small tight, flattened coil in either end of the wire. Attach the legs to the body in the same way.

Lay out Flap Jack so that he is extended *above* the trapeze (not in the normal hanging position) while assembling him. Double the string for strength, and pass it through the two holes in each of the uprights and in each of his hands. Tie the string securely and leave 3/4″ of each end projecting beyond the knot so it will not untie. Flap Jack is now ready to perform. Squeeze the two handles together to see him do his tricks. If he has been strung correctly, there will always be a 180° twist in the strings, regardless of which way he last swung.

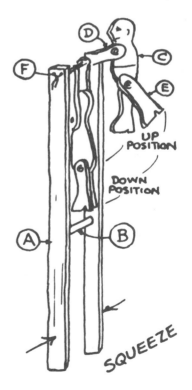

ASSEMBLY

Jumping Jack

(JUMPING TOM OR PANTINE)

This is an articulated wooden puppet held from a string at the top. When a string hanging below is pulled, he jumps (kicks his legs and arms). This is accomplished by a linkage of strings on the back side. Some more recent versions from Appalachia have used coiled dynamite ignition wire (used in coal mining) in place of pins in the leg and arm joints. The figure depicted by this toy may vary; traditional versions have been Jack, a man, and Humpty-Dumpty, an egg-shaped character.

However, the toys were originally called pantines and were imported to America on some of the earliest frigates from France as adult toys.

MATERIALS

1 (A) BODY, wood 4½″ x 3¼″ x ¼″
2 (B) UPPER ARMS, wood 2⅜″ x 1″ x ¼″
2 (C) LOWER ARMS, wood 2⅛″ x ¾″ x ¼″
2 (D) UPPER LEGS, wood 3″ x 1″ x ¼″
2 (E) LOWER LEGS, wood 2¼″ x 1⅛″ x ¼″
1 (F) WIRE, low-voltage hookup wire .060″ diam. OD x 24″ long
1 (G) CORD, braided cotton 3/32″ diam. x 24″ long
  (H) COLORED FELT, 3″ x 3″ x 1/16″ thick
  (I) GLUE, white
  (J) PENS, felt tip, black and red, or PAINT

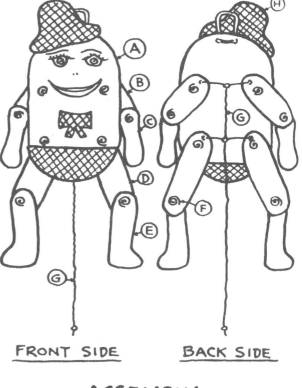

FRONT SIDE   BACK SIDE

ASSEMBLY

Lay out and cut out the wooden items; sand all edges smooth. Drill the required holes. Attach the arms and legs to the body with coils of copper wire instead of pins. Thread a piece of the wires through the proper holes and retain it by making a small tight, flattened coil in either end of the wire. Install one loop of wire through the holes at the top of the head as a handle.

Tie cords between the arms and legs on the backside as shown to provide a linkage terminating in a hanging cord. Use pen or paintbrush to add facial features; also cut out and glue on a felt hat, tie, and pants. Test its action by supporting Jumping Jack with the upper handle while pulling down on the lower cord.

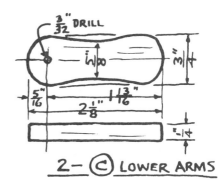

2 — Ⓒ LOWER ARMS

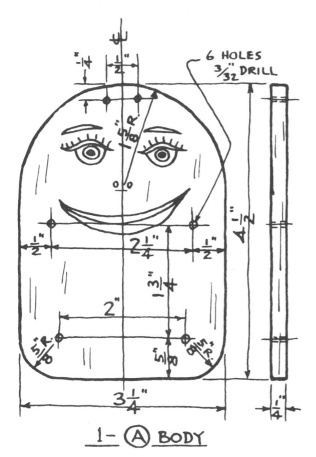

1 — Ⓐ BODY

6 HOLES
$\frac{3}{32}$" DRILL

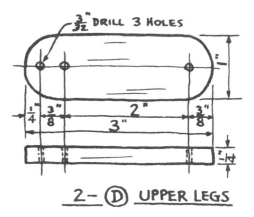

2 — Ⓓ UPPER LEGS

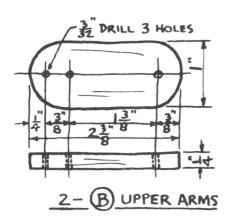

2 — Ⓑ UPPER ARMS

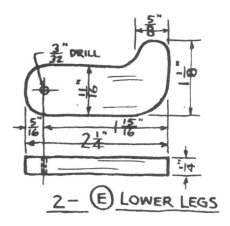

2 — Ⓔ LOWER LEGS

Chickens Pecking

In this animated plaything four jointed chickens peck in 1, 2, 3, 4 order at a pile of corn in the center of a hand board. This is accomplished by grasping the handle of the hand board, often shaped like the ace of spades, and swinging it around in a horizontal plane. A swinging weight below the hand board is connected by four strings to each of the chickens. As the weight swings around, it actuates the pecking order of the chickens.

Another similar toy is the carpenters, which is worked by swinging the weight back and forth instead of around. This one has two figures representing the carpentry trade. The oscillating weight causes one figure to hew wood with a froe while the other uses a handsaw.

MATERIALS

1 (A) HAND BOARD, hardwood 11″ x 7⅜″ x 11/16″
4 (B) HEADS, wood 1 3/16″ x 2″ x ½″
4 (C) BODIES, wood 2 13/16″ x 1 3/16″ x ½″
4 (D) LEGS, birch dowels ¼″ diam. x 1½″ long
1 (E) WEIGHT, smooth stone, approx. 5 ounces
5 (F) KERNELS OF CORN
1 (G) BELL CAP, large size (used for jewelry stone mounts)
4 (H) NAILS, ½″ long
1 (I) STRING, nylon monofilament fishline, 75″ long
(J) GLUE, white
(K) GLUE, epoxy
(L) PAINT, flat black

Lay out and cut out all wooden parts. Drill the holes in the hand board, and countersink the 5/32″ holes both on the top and bottom surfaces to keep the cords from catching on the edges. Glue the legs into the ¼″ holes.

Notch out the heads and the bodies, and drill the nail holes for the hinges on the chickens' necks. Some hand carving is necessary on the chickens' heads, beaks, necks, bodies and tails to give them a realistic look. The eyes are only dots of black paint. Glue the bodies to the legs; attach the four strings to the heads by gluing; then join the heads to the bodies by inserting the nails. Feed the strings through the 5/32″ holes.

With the epoxy glue the bell cap as an attachment onto the stone weight. Tie the four strings together, making sure all four lengths pull equally, then tie the bundle of strings to the bell cap. Glue 5 kernels of corn to the board at points where the chickens can peck at them but will not actually hit them.

Rotary motion of the hand board in a horizontal plane will cause the chickens to peck. The string lengths may need a final adjustment so that all four chickens will move the same.

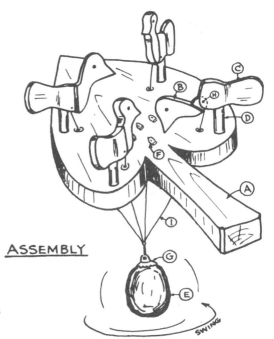

ASSEMBLY

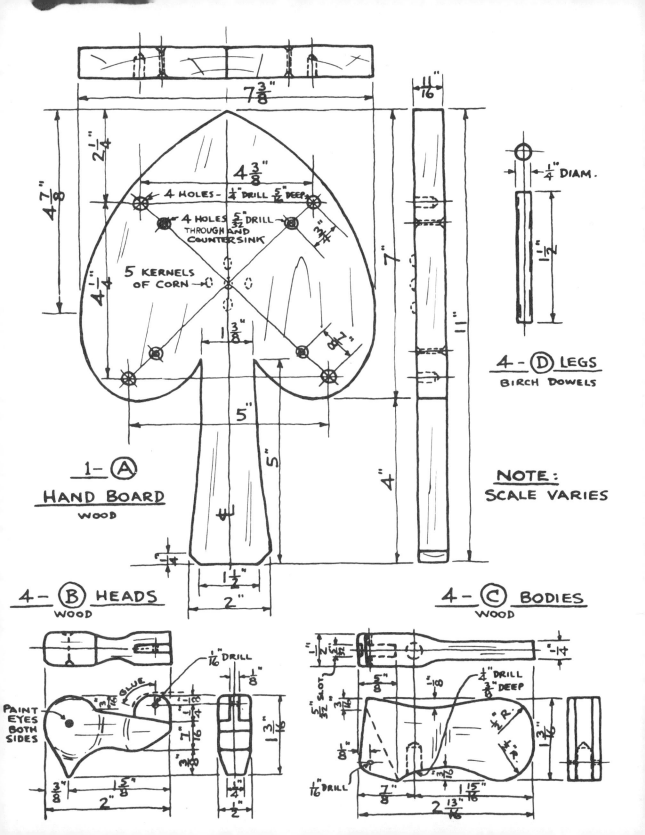

$7\frac{3}{8}"$

$2\frac{1}{4}"$

$4\frac{7}{8}"$

$4\frac{3}{8}"$

4 HOLES - $\frac{1}{4}"$ DRILL $\frac{5}{8}"$ DEEP

4 HOLES $\frac{5}{32}"$ DRILL THROUGH AND COUNTERSINK

$\frac{3}{4}"$

$4\frac{1}{4}"$

5 KERNELS OF CORN →

$1\frac{3}{8}"$

$1\frac{7}{8}"$

$5"$

$7"$

$5"$

$4"$

$1\frac{1}{16}"$

$1\frac{1}{2}"$

$\frac{1}{4}"$ DIAM.

$1\frac{1}{2}"$

4 - Ⓓ LEGS
BIRCH DOWELS

1 - Ⓐ
HAND BOARD
WOOD

NOTE:
SCALE VARIES

$1\frac{1}{4}"$
$1\frac{1}{2}"$
$2"$

4 - Ⓑ HEADS
WOOD

PAINT EYES BOTH SIDES

$\frac{1}{16}"$ DRILL

GLUE

$\frac{1}{8}"$

$1\frac{3}{16}"$

$\frac{3}{8}"$
$1\frac{5}{8}"$
$2"$

$\frac{1}{4}"$
$\frac{1}{2}"$

4 - Ⓒ BODIES
WOOD

$\frac{5}{32}"$ SLOT

$\frac{1}{4}"$ DRILL $\frac{3}{8}"$ DEEP

$\frac{1}{2}"R.$
$\frac{1}{4}"R.$

$1\frac{3}{16}"$

$\frac{1}{16}"$ DRILL

$\frac{7}{8}"$
$1\frac{15}{16}"$
$2\frac{13}{16}"$

Skyhook

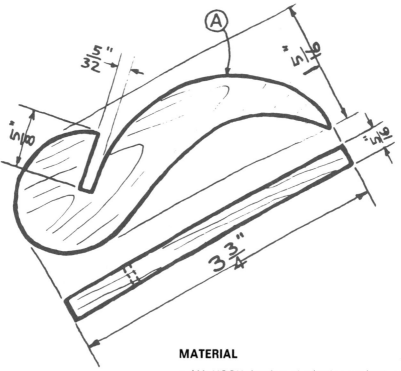

$\frac{5}{32}$"

$\frac{5}{8}$"

A

$1\frac{5}{16}$"

$1\frac{5}{16}$"

$3\frac{3}{4}$"

MATERIAL

1 (A) HOOK, hardwood 5/16″ x 1 5/16″ x 3¾″

Use a jigsaw or carve the wood into the shape illustrated. The edge at the point must be straight, broad and sharp. The skyhook will work with any leather belt, regardless of width or thickness.

BALANCE TOYS

Many people have heard of a skyhook, a legendary device for supporting a weight without any visible means. As with "pulling yourself up by your own bootstraps," few would believe that a skyhook really exists, but it does, and it has been known for generations. A peculiarly shaped small piece of wood, a skyhook will balance itself at the end of one's finger but only if a leather belt is hung in its groove. Nothing but a belt will work, with its stiffness helping to create the illusion that the balance created completely defies the laws of gravity. It looks impossible, and it feels even more impossible when you try it yourself.

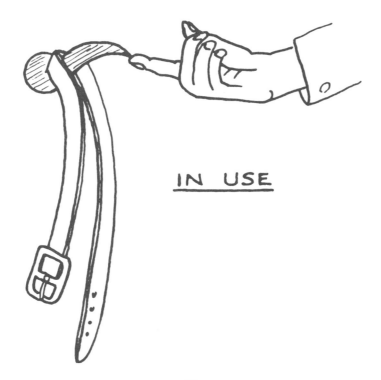

IN USE

Saw Man

(OR SAWYER)

This carved wooden figure, which by weighted balance can perch on the edge of a table, holds an old-time vertical wood saw and appears to be sawing the edge of the table. His balancing is accomplished by a counter-weight (stone, wood or bag of sand) hung on carpet thread extending below the edge of the table and out of sight. When the man is pulled back and released, he is set into the rhythmic sawing action.

A variation of this toy is the woodchopper. He appears to be standing on the edge of a table but facing it while he chops with a broad ax. This one usually has a stiff wire running under the edge of the table and down to the counterweight.

MATERIALS

1 (A)   BODY, wood ¾″ x 2⅛″ x 7½″
1 (B)   SAW, wood 3/16″ x ¾″ x 10⅛″
1 (CR) RIGHT ARM (as shown), wood 7/16″ x 1″ x 2¾″
1 (CL) LEFT ARM, wood 7/16″ x 1″ x 2¾″
1 (D)   WEIGHT, stone, approx. 13 ounces
4 (E)   BOX NAILS, ⅝″ long
1 (F)   CARPET THREAD, 24″ long
  (G)   GLUE, white
  (H)   PEN, fine felt tip, black, or PAINT

Saw all the wooden parts. Hand-carve rounded edges on the body and arms, including the depression at the neck. Drill the holes in the saw and weight, using a carbide drill for the hole in the stone. Nail and glue the arms to the body, and nail the hands to the upper end of the saw, with the saw teeth facing the man and aimed to cut on a downstroke. Add facial features, buttons, and a belt by drawing them with a pen or paintbrush.

Rig a loop of thread around the man's neck, down his back, between his legs and around one of the saw notches. The other notches are for adjustments. Loop another thread through the lower end of the saw and fasten to the weight.

Test the assembly by placing the man on the edge of a table and setting him in motion. Adjust the weight and the thread harness if required.

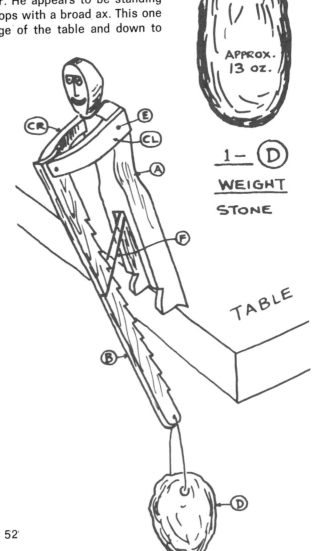

3/16″ DRILL THROUGH

APPROX. 13 OZ.

1 – D
WEIGHT
STONE

52

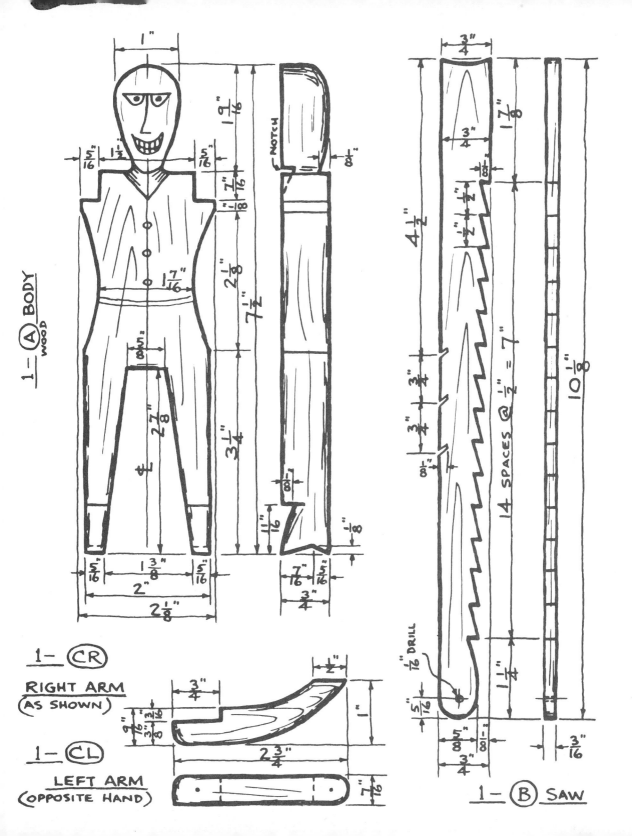

1 — Ⓐ BODY
WOOD

1" · 1 9⁄16" · 5⁄16" · 1½" · 5⁄16" · 1 7⁄16" · 1 1⁄8" · 2 1⁄8" · 7½" · 1 7⁄16" · 3¼" · 2 7⁄8" · 1 5⁄8" · 5⁄16" · 1 3⁄8" · 5⁄16" · 2" · 2 1⁄8"

NOTCH · 1⁄8" · 1 1⁄16" · 1⁄8" · 7⁄16" · 5⁄16" · 3⁄4"

1 — Ⓒ Ⓡ

RIGHT ARM
(AS SHOWN)

1 — Ⓒ Ⓛ

LEFT ARM
(OPPOSITE HAND)

3⁄4" · ½" · 1" · 9⁄16" · 3⁄16" · 3⁄8" · 2 3⁄4" · 7⁄16"

1 — Ⓑ SAW

3⁄4" · 3⁄4" · 1 7⁄8" · 4½" · ½" · ½" · ½" · 14 SPACES @ ½" = 7" · 3⁄4" · 3⁄4" · 3⁄4" · 1⁄8" · 10 1⁄8" · 1 1⁄4" · 1⁄16" DRILL · 5⁄16" · 5⁄8" · 1⁄8" · 3⁄4" · 3⁄16"

Ball Trick

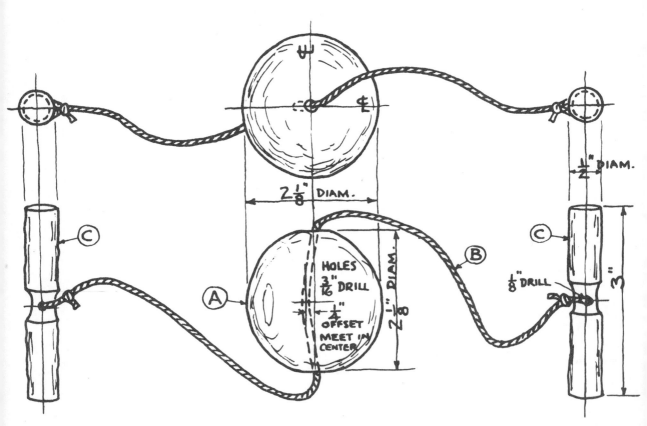

TRICK TOYS

This is an "educated" wooden ball on a string. It can drop down a string in small steps at the operator's command, and it can "count" the steps, leaving children mystified.

The secret is that the hole is not drilled straight through the ball but has a slight offset. When a little tension is put on the string, it will brake and stop the ball; when the string is slacked, the ball will drop again.

MATERIALS

1 (A) BALL, hardwood 2⅛" sphere
1 (B) CORD, hard cotton 3/32" diam. x 42" long
2 (C) HANDLES, wooden branches ½" diam. x
     3" long

Turn the hardwood ball on a lathe. The trickiest thing about making this trick is drilling the center hole. It must be on the center for balance and yet it must be offset, and the two drill holes must meet in the center and without a burr, which could snag the cord. The drilling must be done carefully, indexing and marking the location and amount of the offset, so that the two holes will meet. The hole may be smoothed with a small round file to remove burrs.

Cut the handles to length and grind a groove around their centers. Drill a hole in each handle at its center. Using a wire, thread the cord through the ball. Tie the ends of the cord through the holes in the handles.

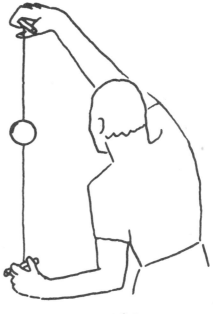

IN USE

Fishhook

(OR IDIOT STICK)

This illusion fools everyone who sees it for the first time. A knobbed stick with a slight hook carved on it is inserted into a hole in a block of wood. There is a rubber band running through the block, and the object is to snag the rubber band with the hook. The operator does it easily, as evidenced by the hook snapping back into the block under the rubber band's tension. However, a novice can't do it at all.

Actually *no* one can do it because the hook is too short anyway and the whole thing is an illusion. The knob on the hook is of such a shape that, when squeezed, it will jump out of one's fingers in a manner that invariably convinces a person that the rubber band has been hooked.

To confuse the novice further, notches can be carved into the knob or block, making him think that the knob must be turned a certain way, as in a combination lock.

MATERIALS

1 (A) BLOCK, hardwood ⅞" x ⅞" x 4¼" long
1 (B) RUBBER BAND, approx. 1¾" long
1 (C) KNOB, hardwood ⅞" diam. x ⅞" long
1 (D) HOOK, birch dowel 3/16" diam. x 2 15/16" long
  (E) GLUE, white

Cut the block to size, drill the deep hole on its axis, and drill the cross hole for the rubber band. After the rubber band has been drawn through the block, secure the rubber band by tying an overhand knot in it on either side.

Turn the knob on a lathe, and give it a high polish by buffing. Drill the knob to receive the hook stick. Cut the hook stick to length, point its end, carve the barbed hook notch, and glue the stick into the knob. The overall length should not quite permit the hook stick to touch the rubber band.

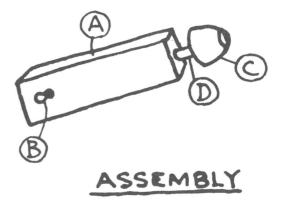

ASSEMBLY

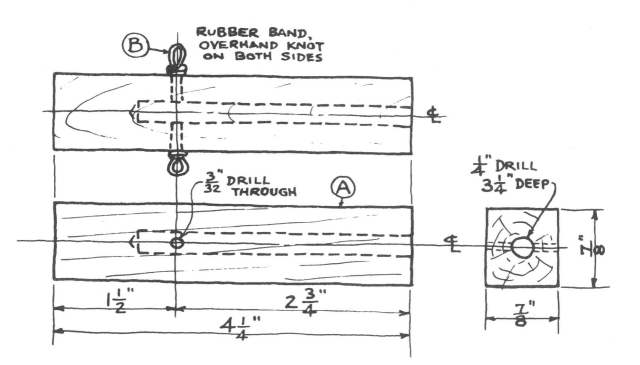

RUBBER BAND,
OVERHAND KNOT
ON BOTH SIDES

(B)

(A)

$\frac{3}{32}$" DRILL
THROUGH

$\frac{1}{4}$" DRILL
$3\frac{1}{4}$" DEEP

$1\frac{1}{2}$"

$2\frac{3}{4}$"

$4\frac{1}{4}$"

$\frac{7}{8}$"

$\frac{7}{8}$"

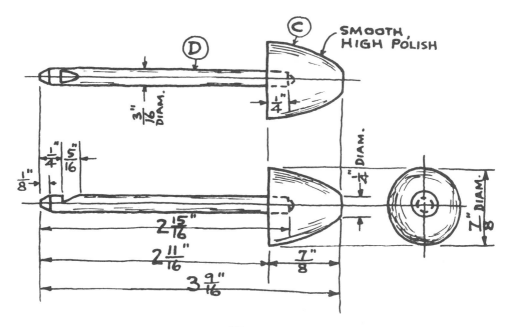

(D)

(C)

SMOOTH,
HIGH POLISH

$\frac{3}{16}$" DIAM.

$\frac{1}{4}$"

$\frac{1}{4}$"

$\frac{5}{16}$"

$\frac{1}{8}$"

$\frac{1}{4}$" DIAM.

$2\frac{15}{16}$"

$2\frac{11}{16}$"

$\frac{7}{8}$"

$3\frac{9}{16}$"

$\frac{7}{8}$" DIAM.

Jack-in-the-Box

Here is an innocent-looking little wooden box. But when the latch on the cover is opened, the cover flies open and out pops a leering puppet much larger than the box. The puppet figure often resembles the characters of the Punch-and-Judy shows. His body is a long but weak compression spring covered with a sheath of cloth. When Jack is compressed into the box and the lid latched, the stage is set to scare the next victim who can be talked into opening the box.

A similar contraption is the mystery box or snake box; however, it has no spring. When the box cover is slid back, a small snake pops out and bites your finger.

As the action of this toy depends on the proper spring, it would be well to make the spring before starting the other parts. It is a weak compression spring, rather well extended, made of .047″ (18 gauge) steel music wire. Make it by winding the wire tightly around a ¾″ pipe (1.050″ actual diameter). When released from the pipe, the spring will expand to about 1½″ in diameter. There should be about twelve to fourteen turns in the spring, and it should be carefully stretched to about 6″ long to make it into a compression spring.

The head is made as a wood turning and fastened to the spring with heavy-duty staples. A cloth dress in the form of a tubular sleeve is sewed around the spring in such a way as to conceal the spring and the staple fastening.

The four sides of the box are cut out, mitered, and fastened together with glue and box nails. The bottom and the top are cut out and are recessed around the edges to fit the sides. For better access the spring is stapled to the bottom before the bottom is installed. Fasten the bottom to the box with nails. The top is placed in position, and the two leather hinges installed, using glue and tacks. The leather hasp is similarly attached with glue and tacks, but with a hole in the leather strap locking over a box nail to close the cover.

Draw a wild face on the front side of the head designed to startle anyone opening the box. To use the box, push the head and spring down, close and lock the top. Anyone opening the box should get quite a shock.

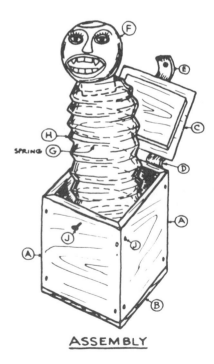

ASSEMBLY

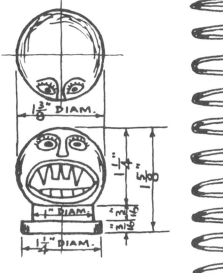

1 – (F) HEAD

WOOD

$1\frac{3}{8}''$ DIAM.

$1\frac{1}{4}''$ DIAM.

1'' DIAM.

1 – (G) SPRING

.047'' DIAM. WIRE, 60'' LONG
(WRAP AROUND $\frac{3}{4}''$ PIPE)

STRETCH TO APPROX. 6''

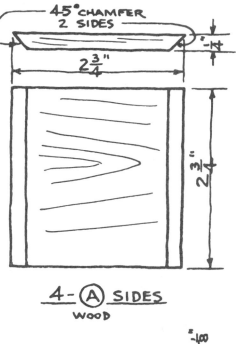

45° CHAMFER
2 SIDES

$2\frac{3}{4}''$

$2\frac{3}{4}''$

$\frac{1}{4}''$

4 – (A) SIDES

WOOD

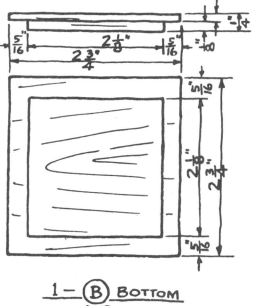

$\frac{5}{16}''$ $2\frac{1}{8}''$ $\frac{5}{16}''$

$2\frac{3}{4}''$

$\frac{1}{8}''$

$\frac{1}{4}''$

$2\frac{1}{8}''$ $2\frac{3}{4}''$

$\frac{5}{16}''$

$\frac{5}{16}''$

1 – (B) BOTTOM
AND
1 – (C) TOP

WOOD

MATERIALS

4 (A) SIDES, wood ¼″ x 2¾″ x 2¾″
1 (B) BOTTOM, wood ¼″ x 2¾″ x 2¾″
1 (C) TOP, wood ¼″ x 2¾″ x 2¾″
2 (D) HINGES, leather 1/16″ x ½″ x 1½″
1 (E) HASP, leather 1/16″ x ½″ x 1½″
1 (F) HEAD, wood 1⅜″ diam. x 1⅝″ long
1 (G) SPRING, steel music wire .047″ diam.
          x 60″ long
   (H) CLOTH, cotton
   (I)   THREAD
   (J)   BOX NAILS, ⅜″ long
   (K) TACKS, ¼″ long
   (L) STAPLES, heavy duty
   (M) PENS, fine felt tip, black and red
   (N) GLUE, white

Pillars of Solomon

A description of the two pillars of Solomon's temple connected by a chain can be read in the Bible in II Chronicles 3:15–17. This account obviously inspired the tricky illusion described here.

A string passes through the two wooden pillars, and it is shown to be whole by being pulled back and forth. A knife is used to cut the string between the pillars, and the pillars are separated to show that it is cut. But when they are placed back together, the string still pulls back and forth. It is all very mystifying until the trickster lets you examine the pillars. Then you find that the cord is actually routed down through the base and the cut string ends were only dummies.

MATERIALS

2 (A) PILLARS, hardwood 6⅝" x ⅞" x ⅞"
2 (B) PLUGS, birch dowels ⅜" diam. x ½" long
1 (C) CORD, hard-braided cotton, 3/32" diam.
       x 18" long
  (D) GLUE, white

The two pillars are to be made identical, especially so that the cord holes, both the real and the dummy ones, are opposite each other.

Hand-carve or hand-turn the two pillars, end bore the ⅜" holes, carefully aligning the holes with the pillars. Drill the ⅛" holes, keeping them smooth and free from burrs. Glue in the dummy cords. Using a thin metal wire for assistance, thread the main cord through the pillars per diagram. Tie an overhand knot in each end of the cord to prevent it from being pulled out. Test the action by pulling the cord back and forth. A little wax on the cord may make a smoother operation.

If satisfied with the action, glue in the plugs to conceal the ⅜" holes.

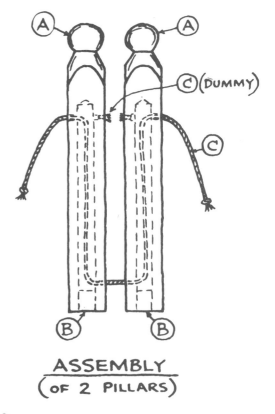

ASSEMBLY
(OF 2 PILLARS)

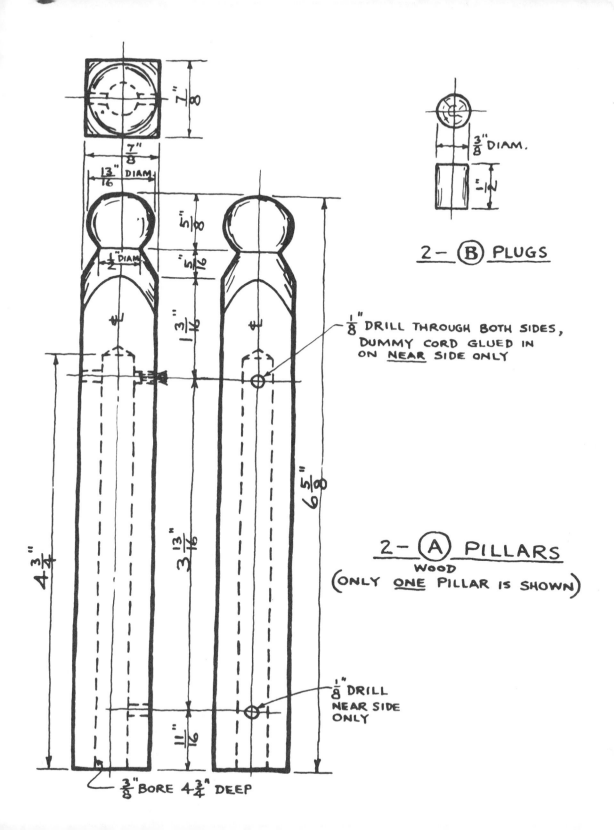

$\frac{7}{8}$"

$\frac{7}{8}$"

$\frac{13}{16}$" DIAM

$\frac{5}{8}$"

$\frac{1}{2}$"DIAM.

$\frac{5}{16}$"

$1\frac{3}{16}$"

$\frac{3}{8}$"DIAM.

$\frac{1}{2}$"

2 — Ⓑ PLUGS

$\frac{1}{8}$" DRILL THROUGH BOTH SIDES,
DUMMY CORD GLUED IN
ON NEAR SIDE ONLY

$4\frac{3}{4}$"

$3\frac{13}{16}$"

$6\frac{5}{8}$"

2 — Ⓐ PILLARS
WOOD
(ONLY ONE PILLAR IS SHOWN)

$\frac{1}{8}$" DRILL
NEAR SIDE
ONLY

$1\frac{1}{2}$"

$\frac{3}{8}$"BORE $4\frac{3}{4}$" DEEP

Beanshooter

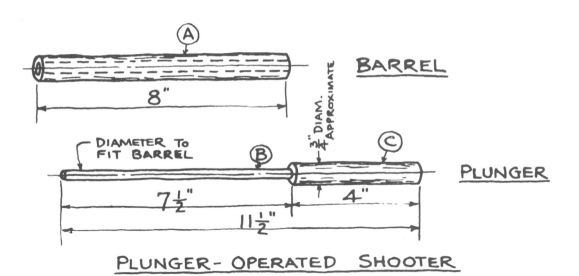

BARREL

Ⓐ

8"

¾" DIAM. APPROXIMATE

DIAMETER TO FIT BARREL

Ⓑ

Ⓒ

PLUNGER

7½"

4"

11½"

PLUNGER-OPERATED SHOOTER

(PEASHOOTERS OR BLOWGUN)

Nothing more than a blowpipe, this toy is made from an elder branch which has been hollowed out. Beans or paper wads are blown through the pipe. Teachers never seemed to like these!

In another version the pipe is fitted with a piston plunger. When a spitball wad of paper plugs the end and the plunger compresses the air, the wad shoots out of the gun.

SHOOTING TOYS

MATERIALS

1 (A) BARREL, elder branch 8″ long
1 (B) PLUNGER, birch dowel to fit, 8″ long (optional)
1 (C) HANDLE, wood ¾″ diam. x 4″ long (optional)

Plunger-Operated Shooter

The barrel is the same as the blowpipe, but in this version a birch dowel plunger is made in a diameter to fit in the barrel. A wooden handle is added for convenience. This works best on spitballs.

Simple Blowpipe

An elder branch is hollowed out with a coat hanger wire or with a rifle-cleaning brush Typical size of the branch is ⅝″ outside diameter, 8″ long. Ammunition can be dried beans or dried peas or spit balls.

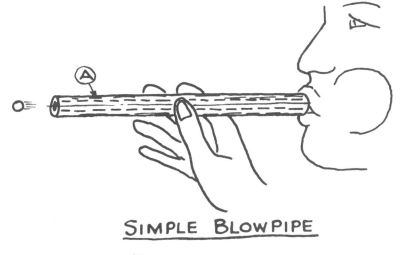

SIMPLE BLOWPIPE

Popgun

This is a safe gun because its bullet is a cork restrained by a string, so it only produces a loud "pop" when the piston handgrip is shoved into the barrel. Pulling back the piston draws the cork back into the barrel to set up the next shot. Working the piston rapidly back and forth causes the popping noise to sound like a machine gun.

The barrel is turned on a lathe and is carefully bored through on the center line. The muzzle end is countersunk to about 45° to assist the cork in entering the barrel. Cut out the handle, bore it to receive the plunger, and sand or file all edges on the handle smooth. Cut the plunger to length.

Make the plunger subassembly by nailing and gluing the cord, washer and packing to the end of the dowel. On the other end of the cord tie and glue the cork. The cord passes through the center line of the cork and through the second washer. The length of the cord from the cork to

the end of the plunger should be 3⅞". The final assembly consists only of pushing the plunger through the barrel and gluing it into the handle.

The most critical part of this toy is to find or make a rubber washer packing which will properly bend to fit the barrel.

To operate, grasp the barrel with one hand, and push and pull the handle with the other hand. The gun will repeatedly load itself, compress the air, and fire the cork.

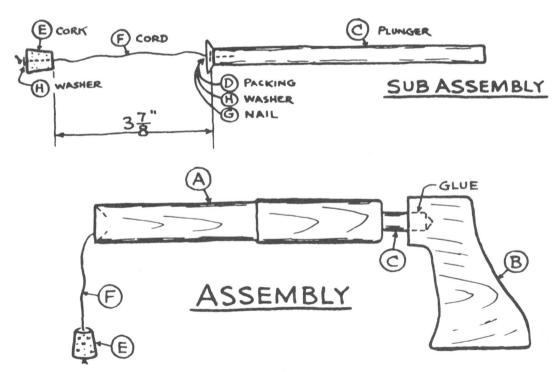

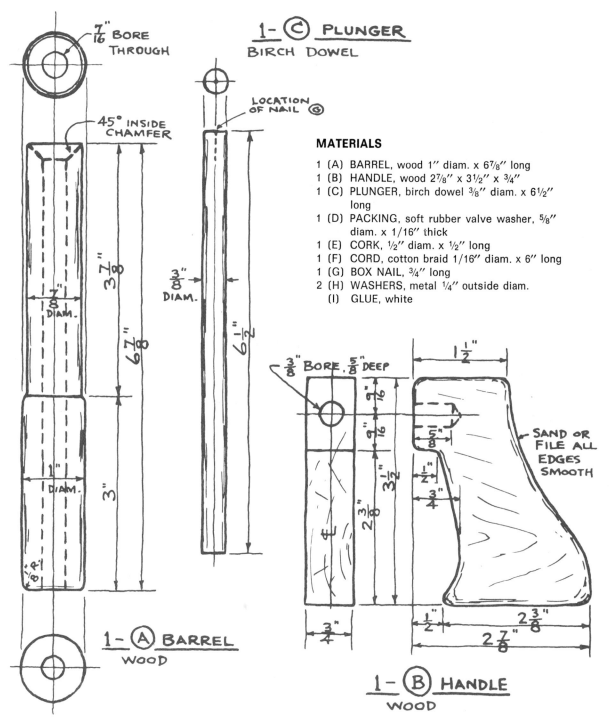

$\frac{7}{16}''$ BORE THROUGH

45° INSIDE CHAMFER

$\frac{7}{8}''$ DIAM.

$3\frac{7}{8}''$

$6\frac{7}{8}''$

$3''$

$1''$ DIAM.

$\frac{1}{8}''$

1 – Ⓐ BARREL
WOOD

1 – Ⓒ PLUNGER
BIRCH DOWEL

LOCATION OF NAIL Ⓖ

$\frac{3}{8}''$ DIAM.

$6\frac{1}{2}''$

MATERIALS

1 (A) BARREL, wood 1″ diam. x 6⅞″ long
1 (B) HANDLE, wood 2⅞″ x 3½″ x ¾″
1 (C) PLUNGER, birch dowel ⅜″ diam. x 6½″ long
1 (D) PACKING, soft rubber valve washer, ⅝″ diam. x 1/16″ thick
1 (E) CORK, ½″ diam. x ½″ long
1 (F) CORD, cotton braid 1/16″ diam. x 6″ long
1 (G) BOX NAIL, ¾″ long
2 (H) WASHERS, metal ¼″ outside diam.
  (I) GLUE, white

$\frac{3}{8}''$ BORE, $\frac{5}{8}''$ DEEP

$\frac{9}{16}''$

$\frac{9}{16}''$

$\frac{5}{8}''$

$\frac{1}{2}''$

$\frac{3}{4}''$

$3\frac{1}{2}''$

$2\frac{3}{8}''$

$1\frac{1}{2}''$

SAND OR FILE ALL EDGES SMOOTH

$\frac{3}{4}''$

$\frac{1}{2}''$

$2\frac{3}{8}''$

$2\frac{7}{8}''$

1 – Ⓑ HANDLE
WOOD

Whiplash

(OR DART)

This consists of a weighted arrow (sometimes carved from a wooden shingle which has a heavy end) with a notch in the side of its shaft. A knot in the end of a short whip cord is inserted in the notch. Holding the handle of the whip in one hand and the tail of the arrow in the other, the user makes a rapid whipping movement. This will fling the arrow a surprising distance. It should always be used in a safe and cautious manner.

MATERIALS

1 (A) ARROW, piece of cedar shingle 17½″ long x 1¾″ wide
1 (B) HANDLE, tree branch, ¾″ diam. x 17½″ long
1 (C) THONG, leather shoelace, approx. 30″ long

Whittle the shingle into the approximate shape illustrated. Many other shapes will work, however, so this can be a source of competition to see who can design the shape that will fly the farthest. Smooth the edges, and cut the notch for the thong.

The handle is made from a small branch with the bark whittled off. Chamfer the ends and carve a groove around one end for fastening the thong. A knot is tied in the outer end of the thong.

To use the whiplash, slip the knot into the notch of the arrow. Holding the handle in one hand and the arrow tail in the other, with a whipping motion send the arrow on a long, spiraling flight.

IN USE

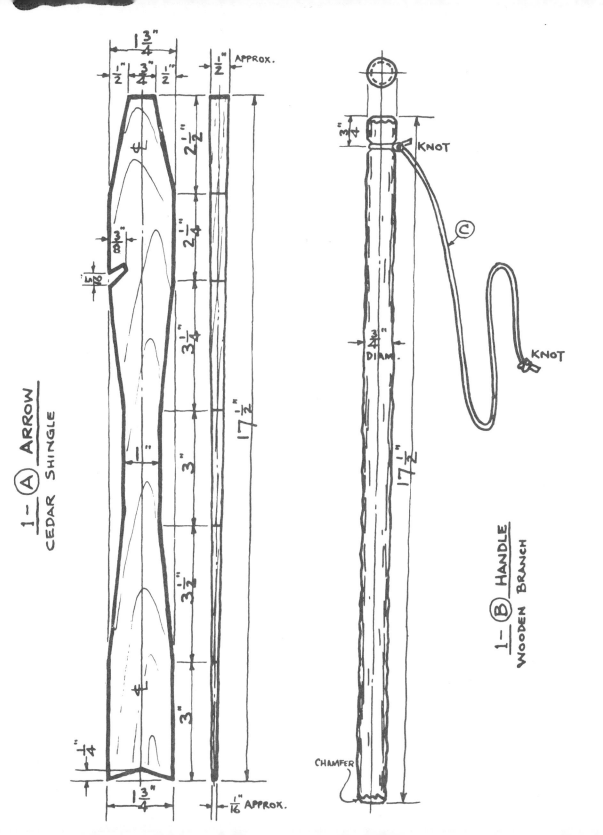

1 - Ⓐ ARROW
CEDAR SHINGLE

1¾"
½" ¾" ½"
½" APPROX.

2½"
2¼"
3¼"
⅜"
5/16"
1"
3"
3½"
3"
¼"
1¾"

17½"

1/16" APPROX.

1 - Ⓑ HANDLE
WOODEN BRANCH

¾"
KNOT
Ⓒ
KNOT
¾"
DIAM.
17½"
CHAMFER

Rubber Band Gun

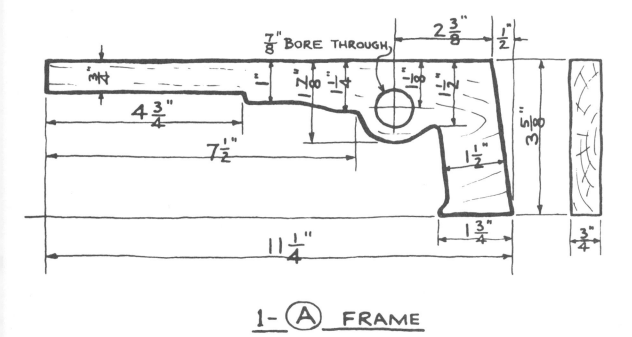

$\frac{7}{8}$" BORE THROUGH

$2\frac{3}{8}$"

$\frac{1}{2}$"

$4\frac{3}{4}$"

$7\frac{1}{2}$"

$1\frac{1}{2}$"

$3\frac{5}{8}$"

$11\frac{1}{4}$"

$1\frac{3}{4}$"

$\frac{3}{4}$"

1-Ⓐ FRAME

With this gun you can zap a fly or a tin can several feet away. It has a wooden frame and a wooden spring-type clothespin for a trigger. The ammunition is rubber bands. Larger rubber bands cut from sections of an inner tube may be used if the barrel of the gun is lengthened to suit. Even a giant cannon can be built to shoot a shell made of several inner tube bands linked together.

Like all shooting toys, this gun has an element of danger. It should be used with care and never aimed at people.

MATERIALS

     1 (A) FRAME, wood 11¼″ x 3⅝″ x ¾″
     1 (B) TRIGGER, wooden spring-type
              clothespin
     2 (C) RETAINERS, wide rubber bands
Several (D) BULLETS, wide rubber bands

    Lay out and cut out the frame, bore the hole, and sand all edges round and smooth. Fasten the clothespin to the frame by stretching two rubber bands around only one leg of the clothespin.

    To load the gun, feed one end of a rubber band into the jaws of the clothespin, and stretch the other end of the rubber band over the muzzle end of the gun. To shoot the gun, just aim and squeeze the grip. The clothespin will open, releasing the rubber band.

    Always be very careful with rubber band guns, which can cause injury.

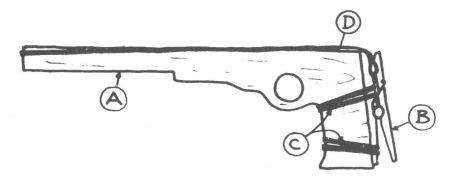

ASSEMBLY

Fly Killer

Although built to be a toy, this actually is a pellet gun and should be used with caution. The barrel is a hollowed-out piece of wood or an elder branch. The power is supplied by a thin but strong bow spring of hickory wood. There is a latch trigger, and the pellets are short pieces of wood. When the bow spring is pulled back and latched and a pellet inserted in the barrel, it is ready to shoot. A well-built fly killer can actually pick a fly off a wall several feet away and may be built strong enough to break a window!

MATERIALS

- 1 (A) BARREL, wood 10¾″ x 1⅜″ x 11/16″
- 1 (B) SPRING, straight-grained hardwood (hickory) 13″ x ⅝″ x ⅛″
- 1 (C) TRIGGER, birch dowel ½″ diam. x 1 5/16″ long
- 1 or more (D) PELLET, birch dowel ¼″ diam. x 2″ long
- 1 (E) WOOD SCREW, roundheaded 1¼″ long
- 1 (F) BOX NAIL, ⅝″ long

Cut out the wooden block for the barrel, shape and notch it, and carefully drill the holes for the bore of the barrel and for the trigger, which intersect. Hand-carve the rounded muzzle portion of the barrel and the open chamber, making sure that the walls of the chamber are smoothly in line with the bores.

The power for the fly killer is a wooden spring made of straight-grained hickory. Cut it to size and taper it. The spring is then permanently bent into a bow shape by soaking it in hot water and tying it into a bent shape while drying. The hole for the screw is drilled.

The trigger is carved from a dowel, with a notch in it to permit a short movement. Pellets for shooting are cut from a dowel.

To assemble, the spring is screwed to the barrel with its outer end resting in the chamber. The trigger is inserted and retained by a nail. If it has been correctly assembled, the trigger will drop down sufficiently to let the spring rest in a cocked position, but when pushed up, the trigger will release the spring.

To operate, pull back the spring to a cocked position, insert a pellet into the barrel, aim, and shoot by pressing the trigger. Again, exercise caution in using the fly killer, since it can be dangerous.

ASSEMBLY

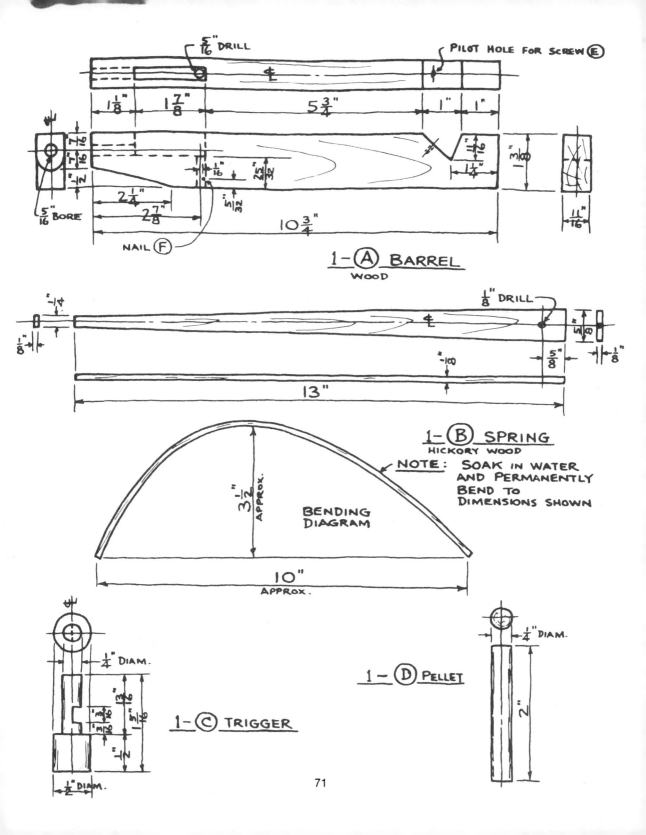

$\frac{5}{16}$" DRILL

PILOT HOLE FOR SCREW Ⓔ

₵

$1\frac{1}{8}$" — $1\frac{7}{8}$" — $5\frac{3}{4}$" — 1" — 1"

$\frac{7}{16}$"

$\frac{7}{16}$"

$\frac{1}{2}$"

$\frac{5}{16}$" BORE

$2\frac{1}{4}$"

$2\frac{7}{8}$"

NAIL Ⓕ

$\frac{1}{16}$"

$\frac{25}{32}$"

$\frac{5}{32}$"

$10\frac{3}{4}$"

$\frac{3}{16}$"

$\frac{1}{4}$"

$\frac{3}{4}$"

$\frac{11}{16}$"

1-Ⓐ BARREL
WOOD

$\frac{1}{4}$"

$\frac{1}{8}$"

$\frac{1}{8}$" DRILL

₵

$\frac{5}{8}$"

$\frac{5}{8}$"

$\frac{1}{8}$"

$\frac{1}{8}$"

13"

1-Ⓑ SPRING
HICKORY WOOD

BENDING DIAGRAM

$3\frac{1}{2}$" APPROX.

10" APPROX.

NOTE: SOAK IN WATER AND PERMANENTLY BEND TO DIMENSIONS SHOWN

$\frac{1}{4}$" DIAM.

$\frac{13}{16}$"

$\frac{3}{16}$"

$\frac{3}{16}$"

$\frac{5}{16}$"

$\frac{1}{2}$"

$\frac{1}{2}$" DIAM.

1-Ⓒ TRIGGER

$\frac{1}{4}$" DIAM.

2"

1-Ⓓ PELLET

71

Slingshot

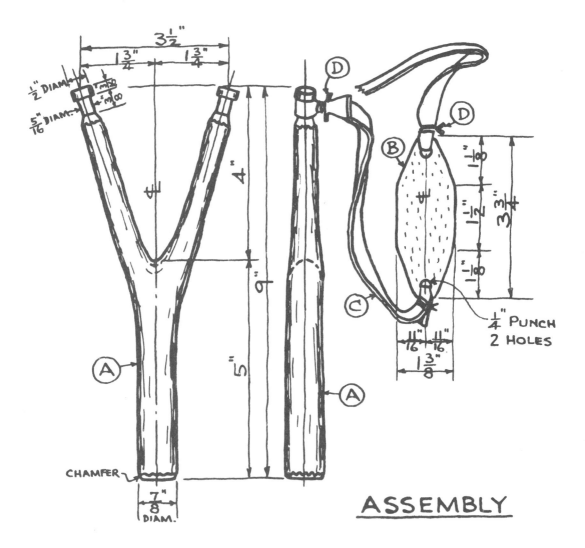

ASSEMBLY

Although common in the past, this toy is in disfavor now because it is actually a dangerous weapon which hurls small stones at great velocity. It is usually made from the fork of a tree branch, with strips of a rubber tire inner tube tied to the forks. A leather pad holds the stone or pebble. When the stone is drawn back and released, the rubber bands propel the missile through the fork opening with great force.

MATERIALS

1 (A) FRAME, forked wooden branch 9" long,
       3½" spread
1 (B) PAD, heavy leather 3¾" x 1⅜" x 1/16"
       thick
2 (C) RUBBER, ½" x 1/16" x 9" long, cut from
       tire inner tube
1 (D) CORD, cotton string, for tying

Select a small Y-forked branch from a strong hardwood tree of the approximate dimensions shown. Shave the bark with a pocketknife. Carve a groove near the end of each fork to help hold the rubber bands. Cut the bands from a discarded inner tube, making sure that the rubber is "live." Cut out the leather pad and punch holes near its ends. The rough side of the leather should be inside to help hold the pebble being shot. In tying the rubber bands to the frame and to the pad, stretch the bands and wrap and tie them tightly with cord.

To use the slingshot, hold the handle firmly in the left hand. Put a small pebble into the fold of the leather sling pad. With the right hand, grasp the leather pad, draw it back to stretch the rubber bands, aim at the target, and release the missile.

Always use the slingshot with great care, as it can be a dangerous weapon.

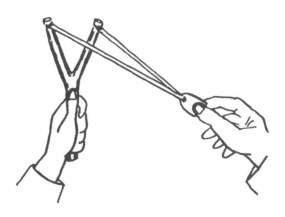

IN USE

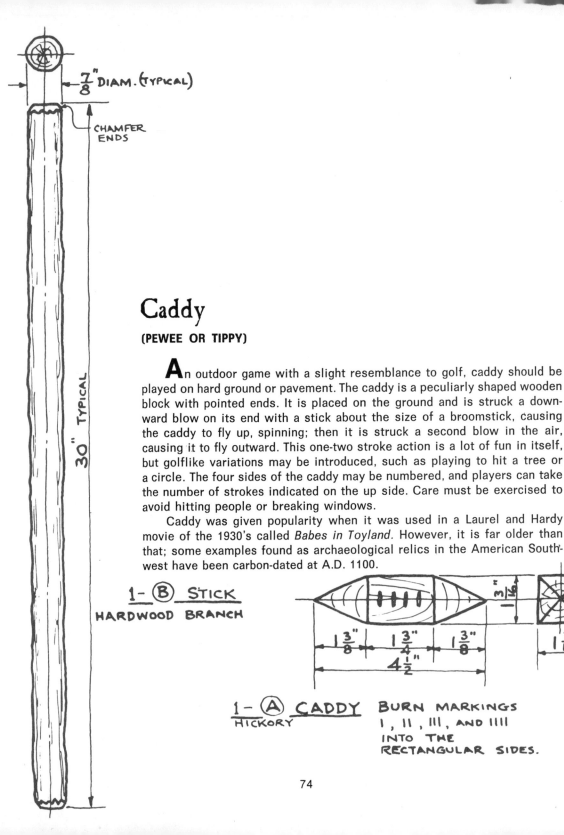

$\frac{7}{8}$" DIAM. (TYPICAL)

CHAMFER ENDS

30" TYPICAL

Caddy

(PEWEE OR TIPPY)

An outdoor game with a slight resemblance to golf, caddy should be played on hard ground or pavement. The caddy is a peculiarly shaped wooden block with pointed ends. It is placed on the ground and is struck a downward blow on its end with a stick about the size of a broomstick, causing the caddy to fly up, spinning; then it is struck a second blow in the air, causing it to fly outward. This one-two stroke action is a lot of fun in itself, but golflike variations may be introduced, such as playing to hit a tree or a circle. The four sides of the caddy may be numbered, and players can take the number of strokes indicated on the up side. Care must be exercised to avoid hitting people or breaking windows.

Caddy was given popularity when it was used in a Laurel and Hardy movie of the 1930's called *Babes in Toyland.* However, it is far older than that; some examples found as archaeological relics in the American Southwest have been carbon-dated at A.D. 1100.

1- Ⓑ STICK
HARDWOOD BRANCH

$1\frac{3}{8}$" $1\frac{3}{4}$" $1\frac{3}{8}$"

$4\frac{1}{2}$"

$\frac{3}{16}$"

$1\frac{3}{16}$"

1- Ⓐ CADDY
HICKORY

BURN MARKINGS I, II, III, AND IIII INTO THE RECTANGULAR SIDES.

GAMES

MATERIALS

1 (A) CADDY, hardwood (hickory) 1 3/16″ x
       1 3/16″ x 4½″
1 (B) STICK, hardwood branch ⅞″ diam. x 30″
       long

This age-old game has had many variations, including even the implements. The caddy shown is made of a square piece of hickory sharpened to a pyramid shape on the ends by sawing or carving. Some remember making the caddy from a round broomstick sharpened to a cone shape by carving. The stick shown is made from a tree branch. Some will remember the stick being made from a broomstick or from a small rectangular piece of lumber resembling a cricket bat.

The game's many variations include:
1. Two or more players take turns stroking the caddy toward a goal (tree, pole or circle). The player first reaching the goal is the winner.
2. Or the player reaching the goal in the fewest strokes is the winner.
3. Or, as the four sides of the caddy are numbered one to four, the side up can indicate the number of strokes permitted after the first stroke.

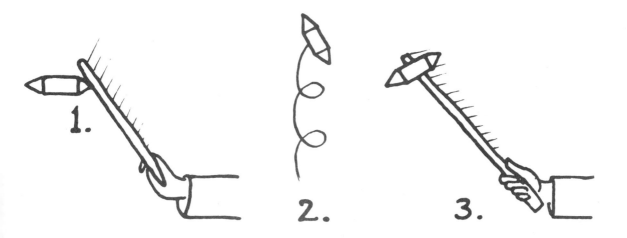

Put and Take

MATERIALS

1 (A) SPINNER, hardwood 1″ x 1″ x 2¼″
   (B) BEANS, dry lima beans
   (C) PAINT, flat black

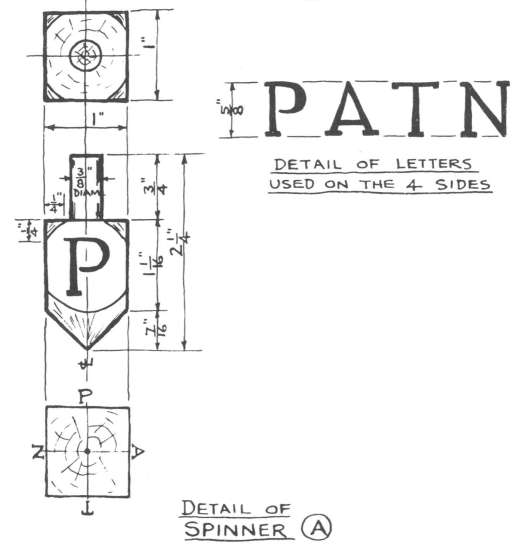

DETAIL OF LETTERS
USED ON THE 4 SIDES

DETAIL OF
SPINNER (A)

This is a gambling game, so to take the risks out of it, we'll play it using dried beans instead of pennies. The gambling device is a small hand spinning top which has four square faces labeled P, T, A, and N. Each time it is spun, it will eventually slow down and fall onto one of its four faces. The letter showing on the side facing up tells the player what to do = Put, Take, All or Nothing.

Put and Take is a game with an ancient origin. The square-faced spinning top has long been known as a teetotum, deriving its name from the Latin *T-totum*, meaning that the side marked T won the entire stake.

The spinner is hand-turned on a lathe or could be hand-carved if carefully done. In any event, the spinner must be carefully centered and balanced so that all four sides have an equal chance of turning up.

A perfectly square piece of wood is chucked exactly on its center and turned to the dimensions shown. If a lathe faceplate is not used, it may be necessary to hand-carve the point of the spinner after removing the piece from the lathe. The four letters are painted on the sides.

Dry lima beans, available in grocery stores, may be used for money in the game.

To play the game, each participant starts with twelve beans. Each antes (advances) one bean into the pot. The first player spins the top and gets his instructions by chance. "Put" means to put one bean in the pot. "Take" means to take one bean from the pot. "All" means to take *all* the beans from the pot. "Nothing" means no action. Turns are taken in order by all players. Whenever all the beans are gone from the pot, it is time to ante again and proceed. Anyone who runs out of beans is out of the game. The game proceeds until only one person has all the beans and he is the winner.

Beanbags

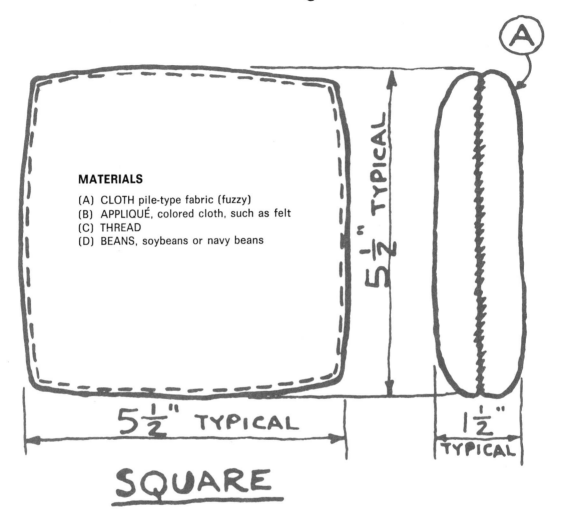

MATERIALS

(A) CLOTH pile-type fabric (fuzzy)
(B) APPLIQUÉ, colored cloth, such as felt
(C) THREAD
(D) BEANS, soybeans or navy beans

$5\frac{1}{2}$" TYPICAL

$5\frac{1}{2}$" TYPICAL

$1\frac{1}{2}$" TYPICAL

SQUARE

A good beanbag is one made of sturdy cloth, well sewn, and partly filled with dried beans. Children have fun just throwing them back and forth; but organized games of skill can be devised, such as attempting to throw them into a box or through holes in a large board placed some distance away. Beanbags can be of many sizes and may be shaped and decorated as animals, for example. Plain sturdy ones are made for throwing around; the more decorative ones, such as the traditional clown and girl, are just for collecting and admiring.

A beanbag gets rough treatment in use, so it must be of sturdy construction. The fabric must be strong, the thread heavy, and the stitching well done. The most attractive cloth is pile material, which is soft and gives a furlike appearance to animal character beanbags.

Cut out the material (two sides) in the shape desired. Add face details or decoration to one side, using appliqués of felt or heavy cloth; zigzag stitch the lines. Place the two halves of the bag together (face side inside) and sew together around the outside except for an opening about 2½″ long. Turn the bag through this opening to bring the face side out and to conceal the seam.

The beanbag is to be filled partially with dry beans, either soybeans or navy beans. To prevent the beans from germinating if they should become wet, the beans should be heated in an oven at 200° F for one hour. The bag should not be overfilled or stuffed, but should feel slightly limp and should measure only about 1½″ thick. After filling, close the opening by turning the edges in and hand-stitching.

BEAR

BOY

RABBIT

CAT

Contour Puzzle

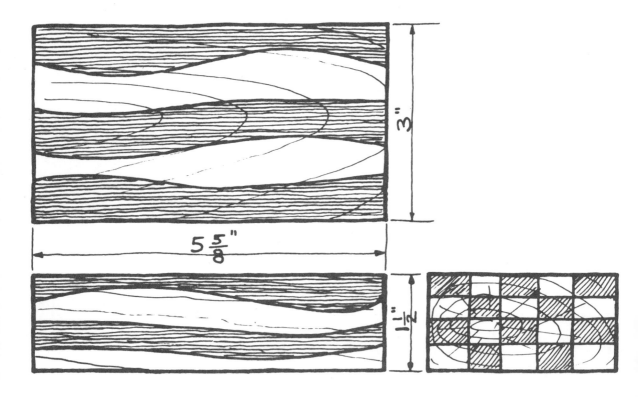

This is a kind of three-dimensional jigsaw puzzle. It is made from a single piece of wood, such as a 2 x 4, which is given random curly cuts with a band saw from two sides. Every other piece has been stained so that the assembly shows a checkerboard pattern on the ends.

The object is merely to reassemble the pieces.

MATERIALS

1 (A) WOOD, clear pine 2 x 4, 5⅝″ long
  (B) STAIN (or paint), *waterproof*, not oil base
  (C) RUBBER BAND, wide

Select a good piece of 2 x 4 lumber free of knots, cracks or other defects. (2 x 4's are not nearly 2″ x 4″ in cross section and seem to be getting smaller all the time!) Cut the piece to length. The sawing of the pieces may be done at random without guidelines. Make the cuts on the 3″-wide dimension first and on the 1½″ dimension last.

Separate every other piece on a staggered pattern for painting. Use a waterproof paint, applied by brush or dipping. Oil-base stain is not desirable, as it may rub off onto the unpainted pieces. When the painted pieces are thoroughly dry, reassemble them with the unpainted pieces and secure with a wide rubber band around the center.

A smaller puzzle from 3″ x 1½″ x ¾″ white pine with 4 x 3 = 12 pieces (instead of 5 x 4 = 20 pieces) is an alternate design.

Ox Yoke Puzzle

This old favorite is very difficult if you don't know the secret but very easy if you do. The puzzle resembles an old-fashioned ox yoke, with a wooden frame and two cord loops hanging from the frame. On each loop is a ring. The object is to move one ring from the right loop to the left loop (so both rings are on one loop) without untying the ends.

The center hole is the key to the solution. By pulling the center knot loops back through the center hole, then advancing the ring through the knot loops, and finally pulling the center knot loops back to the original side, you will find to your surprise that the ring has managed to pass over to the other loop. The ring can be returned by reversing all the steps.

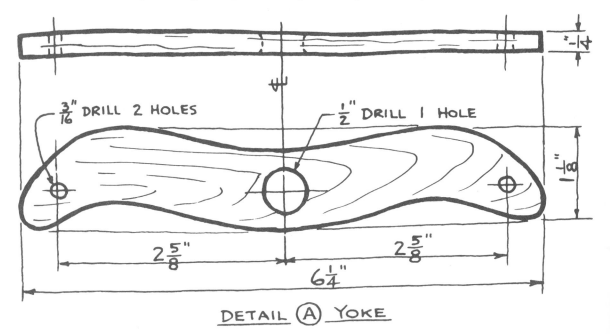

DETAIL Ⓐ YOKE

MATERIALS

1 (A) YOKE, hardwood ¼″ x 1⅛″ x 6¼″
1 (B) HARNESS, cotton cord, ⅛″ diam. x 25″ long
2 (C) RINGS, drapery rings, 1″ outside diam.

Cut out the wooden yoke, drill the one large hole and the two small holes, and sand smooth. Install the cord with the two rings, per diagram, securing the cord by tying an overhand knot at each end.

To work the puzzle, see explanation on diagram.

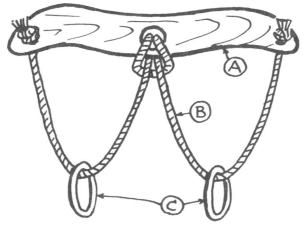

ASSEMBLY

To Work Puzzle:

1. PLACE YOKE SO CENTER LOOP IS BELOW, NOT ON TOP.
2. PULL DOWN CENTER LOOP A COUPLE OF INCHES.
3. MOVE RIGHT RING UP THROUGH AND BACK TO POSITION SHOWN.
4. FEED ENTIRE CENTER LOOP THROUGH CENTER HOLE AND PULL ALL TURNS THROUGH.
5. FEED RING THROUGH TWO LOOPS ON BACK SIDE OF YOKE.
6. PULL ENTIRE CENTER LOOP BACK THROUGH CENTER HOLE.
7. STRAIGHTEN ALL LOOPS, AND RIGHT RING WILL BE ON LEFT LOOP.
8. TO RETURN, REVERSE STEPS.

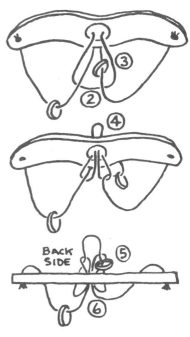

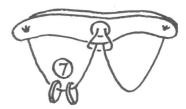

Heart and Clevis Puzzle

This old favorite is made of metal rods or wire. The object is to remove the heart-shaped piece from the remainder of the assembly, and this appears to be impossible. However, with proper alignment of the pieces, the heart can be removed in an instant and replaced just as fast.

MATERIAL

1 (A) BRAZING ROD, brass ⅛″ diam. x 36″ long

    Cut the brass rod into three lengths: heart 14½″ long, clevis 10″ long, pin 11½″ long. Bend each piece into the shapes shown in the diagram. Using a welding torch, braze together the ends of the heart, the two loops of the pin, and the two loops of the clevis (after installing the pin inside the clevis loops). Clean and smooth the welded joints by filing and rubbing with emery cloth. Work the puzzle by inserting the heart, meanwhile checking fits and clearances.

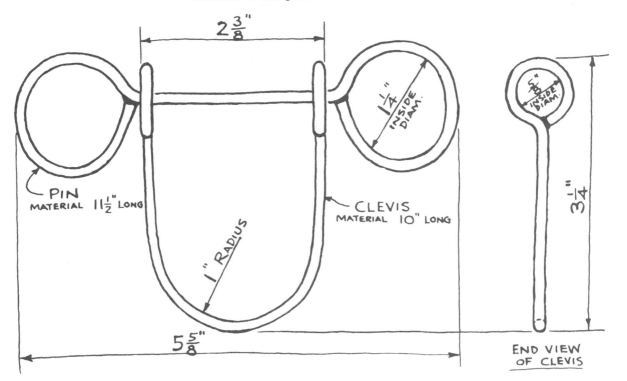

84

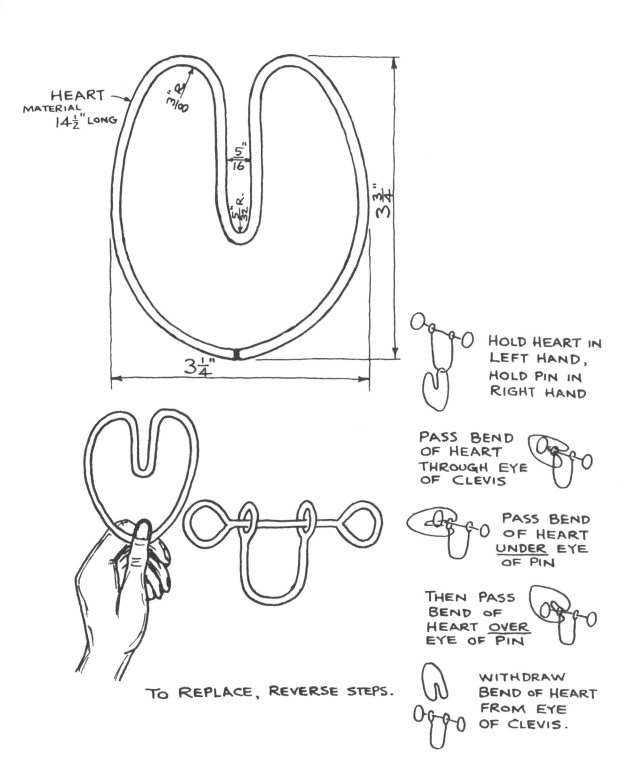

HEART
MATERIAL
14½" LONG

3" R.
3/100

5"
16

5" R.
32

3¾"

3¼"

HOLD HEART IN
LEFT HAND,
HOLD PIN IN
RIGHT HAND

PASS BEND
OF HEART
THROUGH EYE
OF CLEVIS

PASS BEND
OF HEART
UNDER EYE
OF PIN

THEN PASS
BEND OF
HEART OVER
EYE OF PIN

WITHDRAW
BEND OF HEART
FROM EYE
OF CLEVIS.

TO REPLACE, REVERSE STEPS.

Pyramid Puzzle

There are three upright posts on a wooden base. On the left-hand post are seven wooden plates of various sizes with center holes. They are stacked in graduated pyramid order, so each plate is smaller than the one just below it. Using the three posts for intermediate moves, moving one plate at a time and never placing a larger plate on a smaller plate, try to move the entire pyramid stack from the left post to the right post.

The puzzle is not difficult, once the routine of the moves is discovered. It will take 127 moves to transfer the seven plates.

Now for a classical example of the power of arithmetic progressions: How many moves would it take if, instead of seven plates, there were thirty-six plates?

Answer: 68,719, 476,735! Yes, more than 68 billion moves, which, if done at the rate of one move per second, would take 2,180 years! That is why this puzzle doesn't have thirty-six plates!

MATERIALS

1 (A) BASE, hardwood $10\frac{7}{8}''$ x $3\frac{7}{8}''$ x $\frac{1}{2}''$
3 (B) POSTS, birch dowels $\frac{3}{8}''$ diam. x $3\frac{3}{8}''$ long
1 (C) PLATE, maple wood $3\frac{1}{2}''$ x $3\frac{1}{2}''$ x 5/16''
1 (D) PLATE, cherry wood $3\frac{1}{8}''$ x $3\frac{1}{8}''$ x 5/16''
1 (E) PLATE, walnut wood $2\frac{3}{4}''$ x $2\frac{3}{4}''$ x 5/16''
1 (F) PLATE, maple wood $2\frac{3}{8}''$ x $2\frac{3}{8}''$ x 5/16''
1 (G) PLATE, cherry wood $2''$ x $2''$ x 5/16''
1 (H) PLATE, walnut wood $1\frac{5}{8}''$ x $1\frac{5}{8}''$ x 5/16''
1 (I) PLATE, maple wood $1\frac{1}{4}''$ x $1\frac{1}{4}''$ x 5/16''
  (J) GLUE, white

Cut all the parts to sizes shown. Lay out and drill all holes in the base and in the plates. Round top ends of the posts, and glue the posts into the holes in the base. Sand all parts smooth. Place the seven plates on the left-hand post.

The correct sequence of moves will be as follows: Always move the *smallest plate* on *every other move*, going from left to center to right, then back to left to center to right. On the *alternate moves*, make *whatever move is legal* (never placing a larger plate on a smaller one). The puzzle becomes easy, once you know this routine.

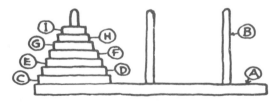

ASSEMBLY

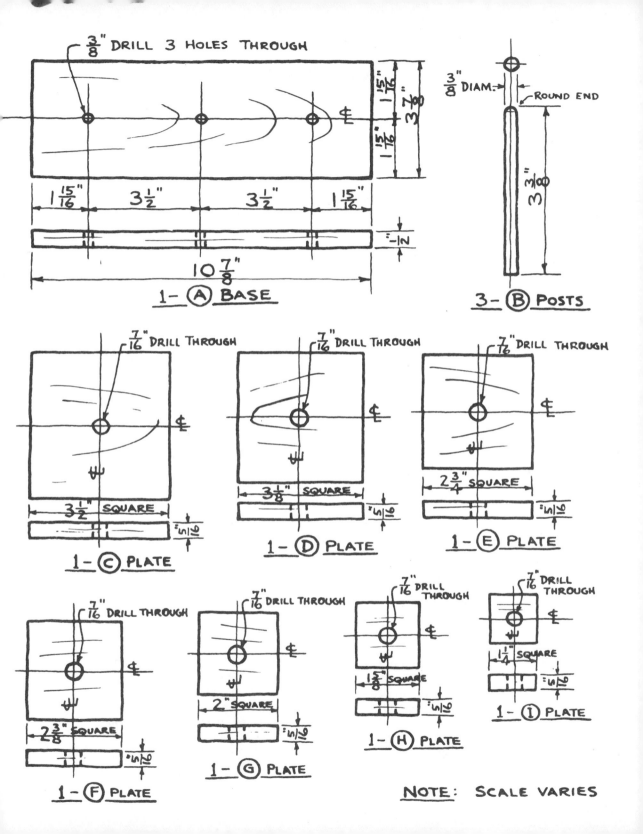

$\frac{3}{8}$" DRILL 3 HOLES THROUGH

$1\frac{15}{16}$" $3\frac{1}{2}$" $3\frac{1}{2}$" $1\frac{15}{16}$"

$1\frac{15}{16}$" $1\frac{15}{16}$" $3\frac{7}{00}$ 3"

$\frac{1}{2}$"

$10\frac{7}{8}$"

1- Ⓐ BASE

$\frac{3}{8}$" DIAM. ROUND END

$3\frac{7}{00}$ 3"

3- Ⓑ POSTS

$\frac{7}{16}$" DRILL THROUGH

$3\frac{1}{2}$" SQUARE $\frac{5}{16}$"

1- Ⓒ PLATE

$\frac{7}{16}$" DRILL THROUGH

$3\frac{1}{8}$" SQUARE $\frac{5}{16}$"

1- Ⓓ PLATE

$\frac{7}{16}$" DRILL THROUGH

$2\frac{3}{4}$" SQUARE $\frac{5}{16}$"

1- Ⓔ PLATE

$\frac{7}{16}$" DRILL THROUGH

$2\frac{3}{8}$" SQUARE $\frac{5}{16}$"

1- Ⓕ PLATE

$\frac{7}{16}$" DRILL THROUGH

2" SQUARE $\frac{5}{16}$"

1- Ⓖ PLATE

$\frac{7}{16}$" DRILL THROUGH

$1\frac{5}{8}$" SQUARE $\frac{5}{16}$"

1- Ⓗ PLATE

$\frac{7}{16}$" DRILL THROUGH

$1\frac{1}{4}$" SQUARE $\frac{5}{16}$"

1- Ⓘ PLATE

NOTE: SCALE VARIES

Nail Puzzle

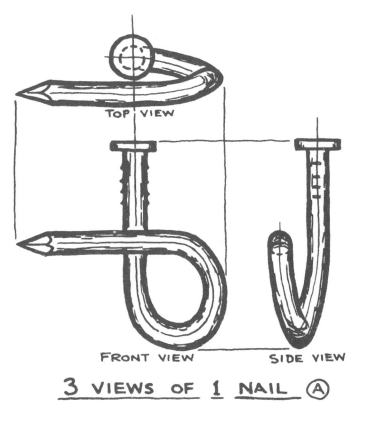

TOP VIEW

FRONT VIEW   SIDE VIEW

3 VIEWS OF 1 NAIL Ⓐ

BEND BOTH NAILS THE SAME, NOT OPPOSITE

Like many good puzzles, this one is very easy, once you know how. It consists of two metal nails or spikes, with a 270° bend in them. They are linked together, and the object is to separate them and then rejoin them. All you have to do is find the proper alignment. It is a good puzzle because just when you think you'll never get it disengaged, it may fall apart, and when you finally think you know how to solve it, you may find yourself embarrassed when you can't demonstrate it to another person.

MATERIALS

2 (A) NAILS, 60-penny nails (6″ long)

Both nails are to be bent into a 270° twist the *same* way, *not opposite* to each other. The bending is done by hammering the nail around a ½″ pipe (actual outside diameter .840″) while the nail and the pipe are clamped in a vise. The gap between the coils of the nail shank must be too small to permit the other nail to pass through (about 3/16″ opening if the nail is ¼″ diameter). This gap may be adjusted by forcing with the vise. When the bending and shaping are done, any burrs which resulted from clamping and hammering should be removed by filing and sanding smooth.

To get the most fun from the puzzle, try to work It without instructions. Diagrams for the solution are shown, if they are needed.

HOW To WORK NAIL PUZZLE :

— HOLD WHITE NAIL STATIONARY WITH LEFT HAND.
— WORK BLACK NAIL WITH RIGHT HAND, GOING THROUGH POSITIONS SHOWN. MOVEMENTS GENERALLY CLOCKWISE TO DISASSEMBLE, COUNTERCLOCKWISE TO REASSEMBLE.

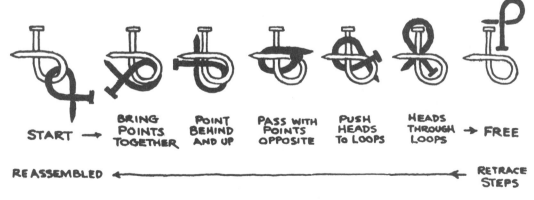

START → BRING POINTS TOGETHER — POINT BEHIND AND UP — PASS WITH POINTS OPPOSITE — PUSH HEADS To LOOPS — HEADS THROUGH LOOPS → FREE

REASSEMBLED ◄—————————————————◄ RETRACE STEPS

Two-Piece Puzzle

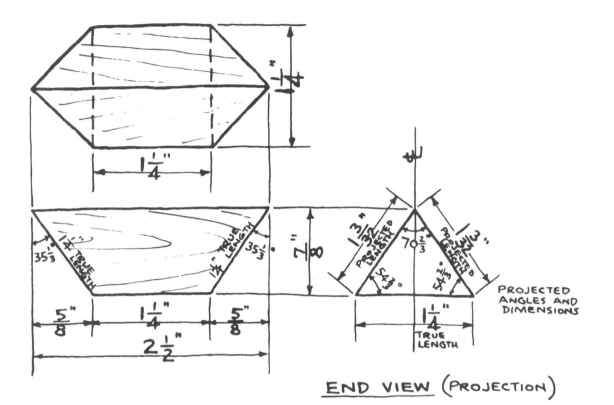

END VIEW (PROJECTION)

MAKE UP A TRIANGULAR BAR
OF THIS CROSS-SECTION AT
LEAST 6" LONG, THEN CUT THE
2 PIECES TO LENGTH.

This puzzle is so simple that it becomes frustrating! Who *can't* fit together *two* simple identical geometric shapes to form a pyramid? Eventually everyone gets the answer, but it takes longer than one would think. The reason seems to be that a person usually tries to fit the two identical pieces together in symmetrical fashion, but the answer is nonsymmetrical. Put the two squares together, and rotate one piece. They make a special kind of pyramid known as a tetrahedron, with all four sides being equilateral triangles.

MATERIAL

1 (A) WOOD 1½″ x 1½″ x 8″

Careful work is required to make this puzzle, as all angles and lengths must be accurate.

Prepare the straight triangular wooden bar from which the two pieces are made, using a bench saw or table saw. Note that the cross section is *not* a 60° equilateral triangle but rather is an isosceles triangle with a 70⅔° apex (top) angle and two 54⅔° base angles.

From this triangular bar cut the two pieces, with 35⅓° angular cuts at both ends, making sure that the 70⅔° apex angle is on top while cutting. Smooth all cuts by sanding. Put the two pieces together to test the accuracy. If the cutting was done correctly, each piece has a perfectly square base, and all surfaces now *are* 60° equilateral triangles.

SOLUTION

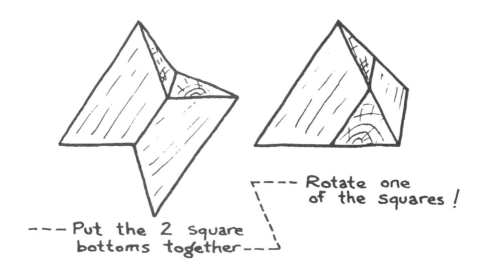

--- Put the 2 square bottoms together---

---- Rotate one of the squares!

Furniture Puzzle

Hardly difficult enough to be called a puzzle, this block of wood has been given nine cuts in an ingenious manner so that, when taken apart, ten pieces of furniture emerge. Included are various sizes of tables and chairs. In a very short time all may be band-sawed out of a single wooden block. Due to the clever interlocking design, there is no scrap except a little sawdust. The individual pieces may actually be used as doll furniture.

MATERIAL

1 (A) BLOCK, hardwood 3½″ x 3½″ x 8″ long

Start with the hardwood block, 3½″ x 3½″ x 8″. The square cross section (3½″ x 3½″) should have rounded corners, about 3/16″ radius. Using a band saw, perform each of the nine cuts in the sequence shown in the diagram. Except where otherwise shown, the thickness of all parts cut is ⅜″, and all radii are ⅜″.

Cut #1 produces a large-size table.
Cut #2 separates two groups for further cutting.
Cut #3 produces a large-size chair.
Cut #4 produces two medium-size chairs.
Cut #5 separates two groups for further cutting.
Cut #6 produces two small-size chairs.
Cut #7 produces a small-size table.
Cut #8 produces a small-size table.
Cut #9 produces a large-size chair and a medium-size table.

Sand lightly any cuts if necessary. Reassemble the block, and keep it together by wrapping two broad rubber bands around the block.

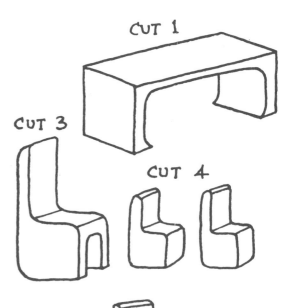

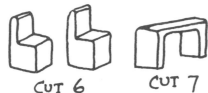

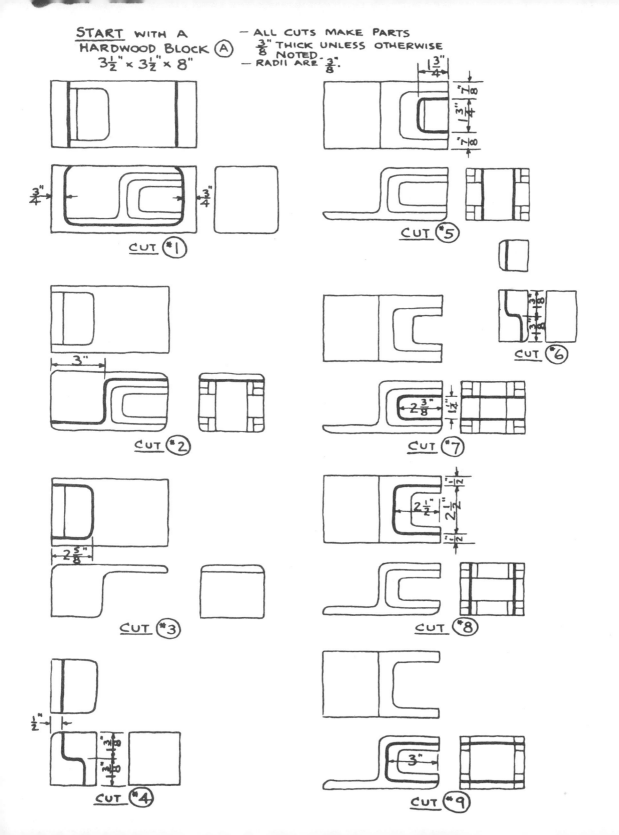

START WITH A
HARDWOOD BLOCK (A)
$3\frac{1}{2}" \times 3\frac{1}{2}" \times 8"$

— ALL CUTS MAKE PARTS
$\frac{3}{8}"$ THICK UNLESS OTHERWISE
NOTED.
— RADII ARE $\frac{3}{8}"$.

CUT #1

CUT #5

CUT #2

CUT #6

CUT #7

CUT #3

CUT #8

CUT #4

CUT #9

Corncob and Cornstalk Animals

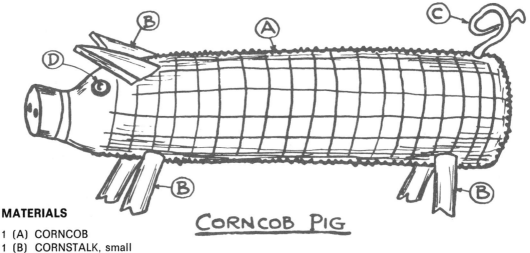

CORNCOB PIG

MATERIALS

1 (A) CORNCOB
1 (B) CORNSTALK, small
1 (C) GRAPEVINE TENDRIL
2 (D) MAP TACKS, black
  (E) GLUE, white

Ingenious caricature figurines can be made from various parts of the corn plant. Typically, pigs, mules, cows, horses and people are carved and assembled completely from corncob and cornstalk material. A grapevine tendril is sometimes added for the twisted tail of a pig. Black map tacks make shiny eyes for the animals.

94

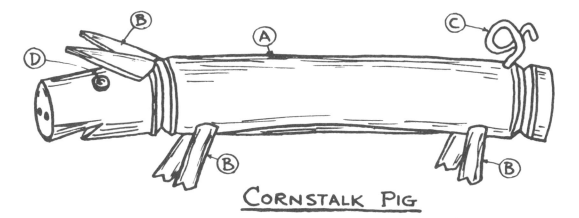

CORNSTALK PIG

CORNCOB PIG

Cut the corncob to the length desired; shape the stem end to become the snout. Drill two shallow holes for nostrils, two holes to hold map tack eyes, four holes for legs, two holes for ears, and one hole for the tail. Install all these items with glue. Shape the ears, and notch the ends of the feet.

CORNSTALK PIG

MATERIALS

1 (A) CORNSTALK, large
1 (B) CORNSTALK, small
1 (C) GRAPEVINE TENDRIL
2 (D) MAP TACKS, black
  (E) GLUE, white

Cut a length of about 1¼ joints of cornstalk as shown, with the ¼ joint becoming the head of the pig and the grooved side of the stalk on the underneath side of the pig. Otherwise, it is made in a similar manner to the corncob pig.

Other domestic animals can be fashioned from the same materials.

COW

MULE

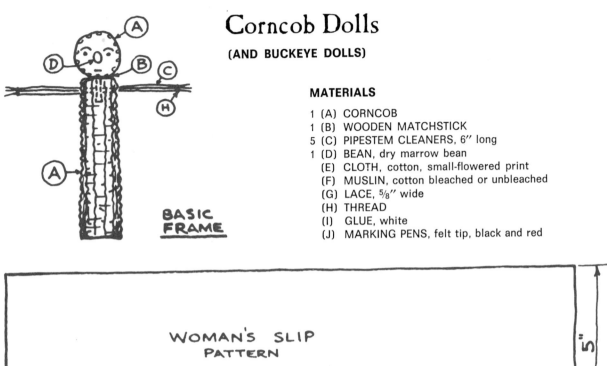

Corncob Dolls

(AND BUCKEYE DOLLS)

BASIC FRAME

MATERIALS

1 (A) CORNCOB
1 (B) WOODEN MATCHSTICK
5 (C) PIPESTEM CLEANERS, 6" long
1 (D) BEAN, dry marrow bean
  (E) CLOTH, cotton, small-flowered print
  (F) MUSLIN, cotton bleached or unbleached
  (G) LACE, 5/8" wide
  (H) THREAD
  (I) GLUE, white
  (J) MARKING PENS, felt tip, black and red

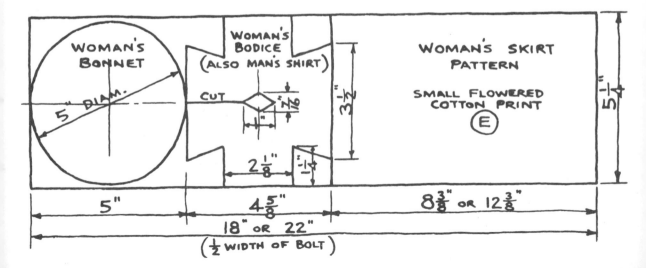

WOMAN'S SLIP
PATTERN
MUSLIN
(F)

5"

18" OR 22"
(1/2 WIDTH OF BOLT)

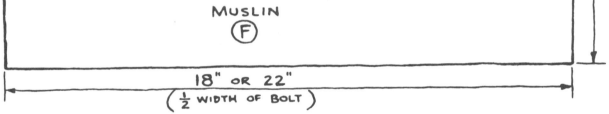

WOMAN'S
BONNET

5" DIAM.

WOMAN'S
BODICE
(ALSO MAN'S SHIRT)

CUT

WOMAN'S SKIRT
PATTERN

SMALL FLOWERED
COTTON PRINT
(E)

5 1/4"

5"   4 5/8"   8 3/8" OR 12 3/8"

18" OR 22"
(1/2 WIDTH OF BOLT)

A corncob can be used for the body of a doll which is so homely that it is cute. A slice of corncob for a head is fastened to the body, and a bean is inserted for the nose. A few facial features are added with a pen or brush, but a cutoff corncob almost makes a face by itself.

Women corncob dolls usually have sunbonnets and long dresses, while the men wear overalls. A tiny baby for the woman can be made from a nubbin corncob.

A variation of the corncob doll is the buckeye doll. It has a corncob body, but the head is a buckeye nut, which has a dark-brown color, so it becomes a black doll. Again, a tiny buckeye nut and a nubbin corncob will make a buckeye baby doll.

Cut off about 1" of the large end of a corncob for the head, and use the remainder of the cob for the body. A hole is drilled through the body to receive the arms, while other holes are drilled in the head for the nose and in the head and body for the neck dowel. Applying glue to the entire neck area, glue in the neck dowel, which is just a wooden matchstick with the matchhead removed. Glue in a marrow bean for the nose; draw in the face with marking pens, black for eyes and eyebrows, red for the mouth.

Pass five pipestem cleaners through the body for the arms, and secure with glue. Tie the pipestem cleaners together with thread about 5/8" from each end. Now the basic frame of the doll is done, and it may be dressed in various ways.

If the doll is to be a woman, her slip (underdress) is made from a strip of muslin 5" x 1/2 the width of a bolt (or 18" to 22" long). The slip can be hemmed for a neat doll or left with a torn edge if desired. The waist of the slip is gathered on a sewing machine, and the slip is wrapped around the body and secured by sewing. The entire skirt, bodice, and sunbonnet may be made from a strip of small-figured cloth 5¼" x 1/2 the width of a bolt (or 18" to 22" long). Cut out the parts per pattern illustration, hem the skirt, gather the waist, and sew on. Slip on the bodice, sew it together under the arms and down the sides, and sew the bodice and skirt together. Down the front of the bodice and around the cuffs of the sleeves also sew lace, which, besides being

decorative, helps conceal the raw edges of the cloth. Sew lace all around the edge of the bonnet piece and gather the edge with a drawstring thread near the edge. Tie the thread around the head and further secure the edges of the bonnet with glue. The back of the bonnet is not glued so that it may puff out. The ends of the pipestem cleaners are now fanned out to make fingers on the hands, and the arms are bent into elbows for any posture desired. In order for the doll to stand up, the corncob should be about 1" shorter than the dress. If it is too long, it can be shortened to permit the doll to rest part of its weight on the dress.

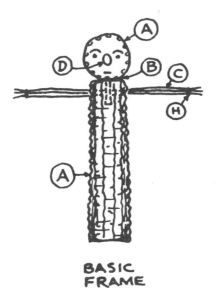

**BASIC
FRAME**

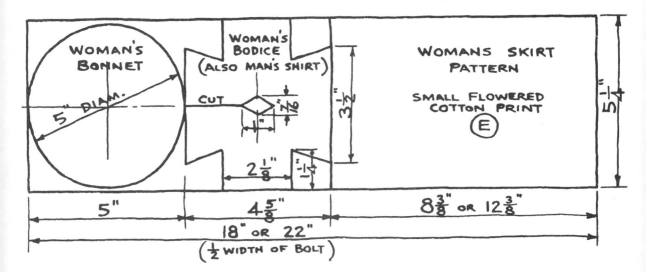

WOMAN'S
BONNET

5" DIAM.

WOMAN'S
BODICE
(ALSO MAN'S SHIRT)

CUT

$\frac{7}{16}$"

$\frac{1}{4}$"

$3\frac{1}{2}$"

$2\frac{1}{8}$"

$-1\frac{1}{4}$"

WOMAN'S SKIRT
PATTERN

SMALL FLOWERED
COTTON PRINT
Ⓔ

$5\frac{1}{4}$"

5"

$4\frac{5}{8}$"

$8\frac{3}{8}$" OR $12\frac{3}{8}$"

18" OR 22"

($\frac{1}{2}$ WIDTH OF BOLT)

Additional material for man doll
        CLOTH, blue denim (overalls)
        CLOTH, checkered (shirt)
        BURLAP (hat)
        STICK, wooden (cane)

Additional material for baby doll
        CLOTH, flannel
        SAFETY PIN, small brass

    If the doll is to be a man, the corncob body
must be split by sawing about 3″ up so that overall
pants can be fitted around the legs. Also, the
legs are notched for the feet. Otherwise, the basic
body is the same as for the woman. To dress
him, the shirt is cut to the same pattern as the
bodice for the woman, but it should have a small
checkered-print pattern. The overalls are made
from two pieces of used blue denim seamed together, and more denim is used to improvise the
bib top and shoulder straps for the overalls.
These can be sewed or glued together but do not
require hemming. A straw hat is made by cutting
a 3″-diameter circle of burlap from a used feed
bag, bunching and gluing it to the head, then
gluing on a narrow hatband of denim. A twig walking stick ⅛″ diameter x 5¼″ long should be
glued into the man's palm so that he can stand
erect.

    The baby doll is made similar to the woman
except from a tiny corncob, and a smaller navy
bean is substituted for the marrow bean nose.
The arms are made of only one pipestem cleaner
shortened to 3″ long, instead of the five pipestem
cleaners on the woman. The baby's only clothing
is a 6″ square of flannel wrapped around it and
secured by a small brass safety pin.

BABY

MAN

Corn Husk Dolls

These traditional dolls were originally made by the Indians, who taught our earliest settlers the technique. The dolls are about 8″ tall and are made from dried corn husks. The skirt has several layers and is cut off square at the bottom so the doll will stand by itself. The hair, either flowing or braided, is made of corn silk. Accessories, also made of corn husks, include bags, brooms, babies, and braided hats. The corn husks are worked wet, similar to basketmaking. The husks may be of natural color or dyed. Facial features may be drawn in with a pen but sometimes are omitted entirely. Occasionally a corn husk doll is fitted with the head of an apple doll for an attractive combination.

Husks are always worked wet. Soak for five minutes before using, and rewet as needed. For the inside of the head, tear husk into ¼″-wide strips, roll into a ¾″-diameter ball, and hold with a pin. For the inside of the body, roll up a similar ball, except 1″ in diameter. For arms, wrap up a pipestem cleaner inside a 1″-wide strip of husk, turn in the ends, and tie with ⅛″-wide strips of husk. Use the clean inside surface of a husk for the face, bringing a strip smoothly over the front but twisting it three times before bringing it down the back. Tie with string around the neck and let the excess husk hang down about 3½″ at both ends. Put arms through between husks and continue to cover body with the same husk and tie again. Split the husk ends. Make a skirt by gathering the narrow ends of several husks around the waist with the curved part at the bottom turned inward. Add more husks until the fullness is as desired, and tie in place with two wraps of string. Trim off surplus ½″ above tie at waist; cut and trim evenly at the skirt bottom. This is the basic doll, and from this point many variations can be made.

The doll needs a blouse, bodice, or shawl, any of which may be made by draping or tailoring wide strips of husk down over the shoulders in front and back to conceal the tied strings. A narrow belt of husk tied around the waist secures the blouse.

Corn silk for the hair also must be soaked for five minutes before using. The hair may be braided into a pigtail, left in a flowing style, or

fixed in other styles. Sew it to the head with brown thread, or glue it. A braided hat may be made of three narrow strips soaked and braided, coiled into a hat shape, and sewed together.

Accessories which can be made of husks include a purse or bag, a baby, and a broom tipped with broomstraw. The eyes and nose are drawn in with a black pen, the mouth with a red one.

If you want to dye parts of the doll, do this before making the doll. Add ½ package of dye and 2 tablespoons of liquid dishwashing detergent to 1½ gallons of boiling water. Place a few corn husks in the boiling solution for fifteen minutes, stirring occasionally. Remove husks, rinse in cold water, and dry on newspapers.

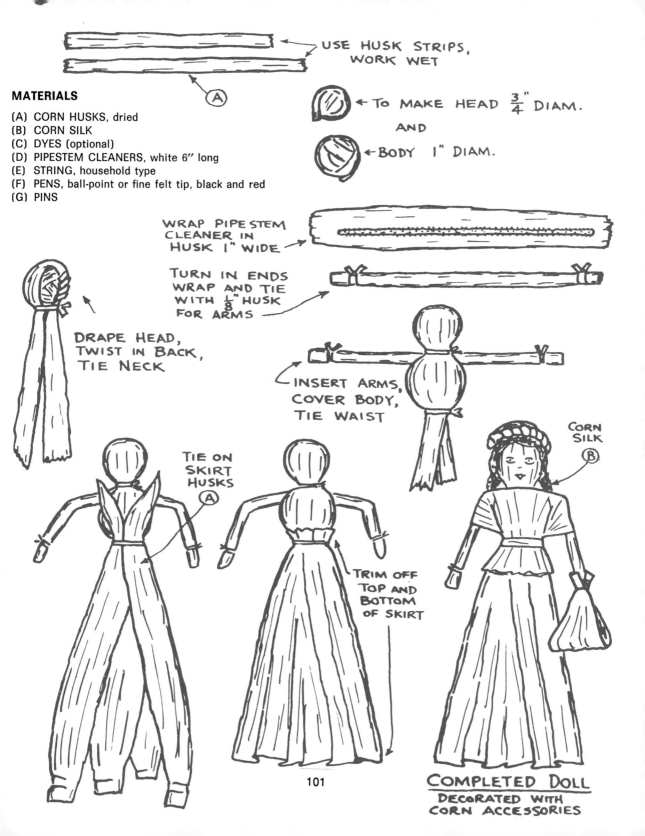

USE HUSK STRIPS, WORK WET

MATERIALS

(A) CORN HUSKS, dried
(B) CORN SILK
(C) DYES (optional)
(D) PIPESTEM CLEANERS, white 6″ long
(E) STRING, household type
(F) PENS, ball-point or fine felt tip, black and red
(G) PINS

TO MAKE HEAD $\frac{3}{4}$″ DIAM.

AND

BODY 1″ DIAM.

WRAP PIPESTEM CLEANER IN HUSK 1″ WIDE

TURN IN ENDS WRAP AND TIE WITH $\frac{1}{8}$″ HUSK FOR ARMS

DRAPE HEAD, TWIST IN BACK, TIE NECK

INSERT ARMS, COVER BODY, TIE WAIST

TIE ON SKIRT HUSKS (A)

TRIM OFF TOP AND BOTTOM OF SKIRT

CORN SILK (B)

101

COMPLETED DOLL
DECORATED WITH CORN ACCESSORIES

Apple Dolls

The head and sometimes the hands of these dolls are made from a dried apple, the balance of the body being of other materials and usually dressed in cotton. The apple head is peeled, and the rough features of the face are carved in. As the head dries, shrinkage and wrinkles give the appearance of character and old age. Sometimes the apple stem is left on, and occasionally the apple skin may be slit and left on to represent hair. Dried apple head dolls are surprisingly durable if they are kept in a dry place, some having been known to last for more than fifty years.

A doll of similar appearance is the dough head doll. The head of this one is molded from dough made of salt, cornstarch, sawdust and water.

Since apple dolls are made in so many sizes and shapes and by so many different methods, it is difficult to advise the best way and to supply patterns that will fit. Because of this, the instructions here are only general.

Select a cooking apple of medium size, remembering that the dimensions of the head will shrink ⅓ or more while drying. Peel the apple, select a good side, and start sculpting. As the nose is the most predominant feature, work around it as a starting point. Make deep slashes on either side of the nose, below it, and also cut above it for the eye area between the forehead and the nose. Cut depressions for the eyes, and shape out the chin at the sides and back to the neck. Make a deep mouth cut, which can be turned down a little to scowl or up to smile, depending on the character you have in mind. Finally add a few light cuts as the start of wrinkles, which will further develop during drying. These wrinkle cuts are in the forehead, around the mouth, and crow's-feet wrinkles at the corners of the eyes.

Preservation treatments vary widely. Among those used are: (a) Soak in a saturated salt solution for 45 minutes and drain; (b) soak in undiluted lemon juice for 1 hour and drain; and (c) expose to a lighted sulphur fumigating candle for 1 hour inside a cardboard carton. However it is done, following the treatment it is necessary to hang the apple on a wire run through the core without touching any other object and to keep it in a warm but ventilated place for at least one month. As it drys, it will shrink and accentuate the wrinkles. When dry, insert whole cloves for eyes (these help in preservation, too) and apply rouge lightly to the cheeks. Apple hands, if desired, may be made and dried along with the head.

The body for most apple dolls consists of an armature made of cloth-wrapped wire. The frame is made by bending a long stovepipe wire in the middle (the head spike), twisting it several times (neck), spreading it out and doubling back (arms), twisting together (chest), dropping down and twisting together again (stomach), spreading out and doubling back (legs), and anchoring near the stomach. The size of the figure should be proportional to the dried head. The armature is filled out by wrapping strips of rags or bias tape around the body, using pink cloth around the arms and other exposed areas and black cloth around the legs. Suitable clothing may be made for the doll and then filled out with cotton stuffing in the bust and hip areas as it is sewed on. Elaborate details may be added to the dress, such as pantaloons, collar, shoes, purse, shawl, hat, umbrella, cotton for hair, a basket, broom, and baby. A man can have overalls (made of used overalls), a bandanna handkerchief, and a burlap straw hat.

The dried apple head and hands are impaled and glued onto the armature. Dried apple dolls should always be stored in an airy place and not handled excessively.

APPLE WITH ROUGH CUTS

APPLE WITH DETAIL CUTS

APPLE, DRIED

MATERIALS

1 (A) APPLE, cooking apple, medium size
  (B) WIRE, stovepipe wire
  (C) STUFFING, cotton
  (D) WRAPPING, strips of rags or bias tape
  (E) CLOTH, cotton, various colors
  (F) DECORATION, yarn, lace, ribbon, felt, etc.

  (G) THREAD
  (H) GLUE, white
  (I) PRESERVATIVE, undiluted lemon juice, salt, or sulfur fumigating candle
2 (J) WHOLE CLOVES

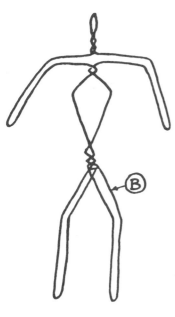

WIRE ARMATURE

CLOTH-WRAPPED ARMATURE

COMPLETED DOLL

Rope Dolls

This macramelike doll is made of jute twine, such as that used for binding or wrapping. The arms and legs are braided, and the hair may be done in a similar fashion. The doll is dressed using cotton, ribbon or lace, which makes a strong contrast with the coarse jute body.

MATERIALS

1 ball (A) CORD, 4-ply unpolished wrapping jute
    1 (B) BAG, made of cotton muslin per pattern
    (C) STUFFING, cotton
    (D) GLUE, white
    (E) THREAD, carpet thread
    (F) THREAD, fine
    (G) DRESS, fine percale, colored
    (H) LACE, ½″ wide
    (I) RIBBON, 5/16″ wide
    (J) FELT, red, light blue
    (K) INK PEN, black felt tip

Make a little bag from two pieces of muslin stitched together per pattern. Turn the bag inside out, stuff with cotton, and sew up the opening. This bag is the armature for wrapping the cord to make the head. Coat the right half of the bag with glue and wrap it vertically. When dry, coat the left half and wrap it the same.

The arms are a braid of six cords (three strands of two cords each, braided) with the length before braiding being about 9″. The ends are secured by tying a ribbon bow, which is then tacked down by stitching.

The doubled legs are a similar braid of nine cords (three strands of three cords each, braided) with the length before braiding being about 12″ The ends are secured by the ribbon bows and sewed.

The head, arms and doubled legs all are sewn together at the center of the doll with carpet thread. Ten to fifteen more strands of cord are glued to the head as hair.

The doll is clothed in a simple little dress, complete with lace trimming and a ribbon bow. Another bow or two may be added as a hair ribbon. A mouth and eyes are cut out of red and light-blue felt and glued onto the face. Pupils of the eyes are drawn with a pen.

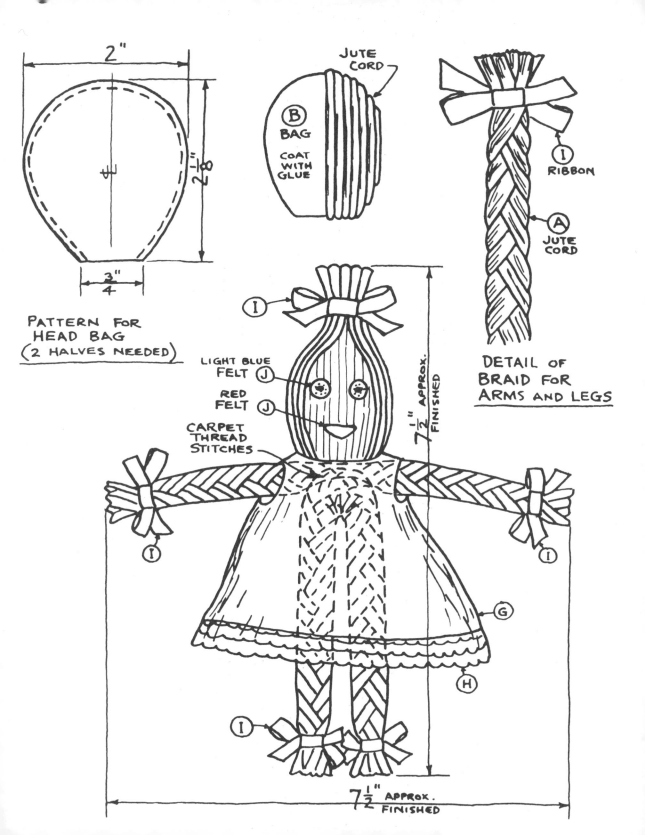

2"

2 ⅛"

3/4"

PATTERN FOR HEAD BAG
(2 HALVES NEEDED)

JUTE CORD

B BAG
COAT WITH GLUE

RIBBON

A JUTE CORD

DETAIL OF BRAID FOR ARMS AND LEGS

I

LIGHT BLUE FELT J

RED FELT J

CARPET THREAD Stitches

I

I

G

H

I

7½" approx. FINISHED

7½" approx. FINISHED

Rag Dolls

The term "rag doll" could describe almost any stuffed, cotton cloth doll made of scraps left over from more ambitious clothing projects. It was a means of using up material otherwise wasted, the same as in patchwork quilt making.

Rag dolls were of many different designs, but most were in the form of a girl with a dress, skirt or apron stuffed with cotton or cloth. The hair might be yarn, and the eyes could be buttons, or the facial features might be embroidered.

MATERIALS

(A) CLOTH, remnants, bits and pieces, various colors
(B) STUFFING, polyester fiber or cotton
(C) THREAD, various colors
(D) YARN, hair colors
(E) LACE, other trims
(F) RIBBON, ½" wide
(G) ELASTIC TAPE, ¼" wide

Due to the existence of so many designs from the past known as rag dolls, the instructions here are general. The dimensions and designs shown are only typical.

Cut out two halves each for the body, head, hands and feet. The color of the head and the hands should be a flesh tone; the body and shoes (feet) should be of compatible colors. The doll is pieced together from the various parts, sewing them together on the wrong side on a sewing machine. The doll is one total unit, having only one gap about three inches long along one side. Turn the doll right side out through this opening. Stuff the doll firmly, then sew up the gap as neatly as possible by hand.

The facial features are embroidered, using black thread for the eyes and nose and red for the mouth. Hair can be fashioned from yarn in girl's or boy's styles and sewed onto the head. If the doll is to be a girl, it may have a simple skirt of a color complementary to the rest of the doll and with lace trimming. The skirt may have an elastic band around the top so that a small child can dress it. If the doll is to be a boy, it may be given a pair of pants and a shirt with a collar.

BOY RAG DOLL

TYPICAL FINISHED DIMENSIONS

Sock Dolls

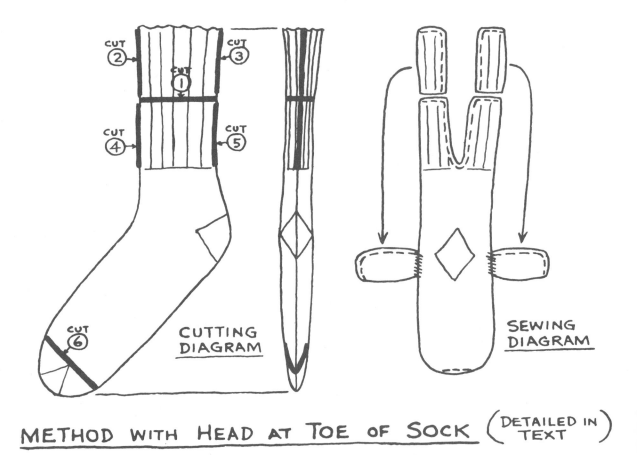

CUTTING DIAGRAM

SEWING DIAGRAM

METHOD WITH HEAD AT TOE OF SOCK (DETAILED IN TEXT)

An ordinary sock may be easily transformed into a cuddly stuffed doll for a small child. There have been various ways of doing this. The toe of the sock, with a little cutting and sewing, can become the feet, and the cutaway material can be sewed on for arms, while the ankle of the sock is the head. Or it can be reversed so that the toe of the sock is the head while the ankle provides material for the legs and arms.

Accessories may include a stocking cap from the scrap, yarn hair, button eyes or an embroidered face, a dress, skirt or apron.

Work socks with contrasting white or red toes and heels are often used. They are particularly adapted to making animal sock dolls such as monkeys and elephants, using the contrasting toes and heels for features like the muzzle of the monkey.

MATERIALS

1 (A) SOCK, man's or boy's orlon (even a baby's)
   (B) STUFFING, polyester fiber or cotton
   (C) THREAD, various colors
   (D) YARN, hair colors
2 (E) BUTTONS, about ½″ diam., color to
      contrast with sock
   (F) CLOTH, cotton, small-flowered print
   (G) LACE, ⅝″ wide
   (H) ELASTIC TAPE, ¼″ wide

With scissors cut off the top half of the ankle portion of the sock, then twice recut vertically the cutoff piece; this will become the arms. Twice recut vertically the remainder of the angle portion of the sock; this will form the legs. Cut off the toe of the sock; this will prepare the stuffing hole at the top of the head and also provide a stocking cap for decoration, if desired.

Turn the sock and the arm pieces inside out and sew the seams on a machine, about ⅛″ from the edges. Turn the parts back to the original side. Stuff the body, including the legs, and the arms with the stuffing material. Fill the doll enough to make it firm but not too fat. Sew up the holes at the top of the head and on the arms. Sew the arms onto the body. Tie a piece of thread or yarn tightly around the doll to form its neck.

BOY

BABY IN WRAPPER

109

METHOD WITH HEAD AT ANKLE OF SOCK

(NOT DETAILED IN TEXT)

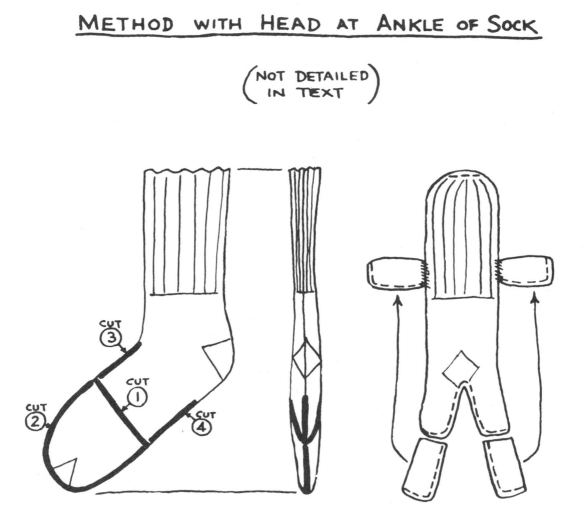

CUTTING DIAGRAM

SEWING DIAGRAM

The basic form of the sock doll is now complete, and it may be decorated in many ways. Eyes may be buttons, except that for babies embroidered eyes might be safer. The nose and mouth are usually embroidered. Hair may be made of yarn in various styles, and the cutoff toe of the sock can be turned and sewed on as a cap.

If the doll is to be a girl, it should have a simple cloth skirt with an elastic band sewed around the waist. A child can easily dress the doll with this kind of skirt. Lace or other decorations may be added to the skirt. If the doll is to be a boy, a simple pair of cloth shorts could be used. If the doll is made from a baby's sock, a simple little jacket or a flannel blanket wrapper would be appropriate.

Another method of making a sock doll is .to turn the sock around so that the doll's head is made from the ankle instead of the toe. The procedure is similar to the one already described (see diagrams). This method makes a doll in more of a sitting position, which some children prefer; however, the head and face are in the ribbed ankle area.

No dimensions are given because of the wide variations in the size of socks.

BABY IN JACKET

GIRL

Clothespin Dolls

A wooden clothespin can become the body of a well-dressed little doll. A good seamstress can make beautiful dresses and suits, arrange yarn for hair, and paint in facial features on the head of the clothespin.

MATERIALS

1 (A) CLOTHESPIN, round wooden type, 3¾″ long
1 (B) PIPESTEM CLEANER, 6″ long
  (C) YARN, in hair colors
  (D) CLOTH, fine white percale
  (E) CLOTH, cotton small-flowered print
  (F) LACE, ¼″ wide, fine
  (G) LACE, ½″ wide, fine
  (H) RIBBON, ¼″ wide
  (I) GLUE, white
  (J) PENS, fine-line ball-point, black and red
  (K) THREAD

Flatten one side of the head of the clothespin by filing and sanding, to become the face. On this surface, draw in the eyes and nose with a fine black pen and the mouth with a fine red pen. Glue a pipestem cleaner around the body, bend out for arms, and bend back ¼″ of each end to represent hands. Cut six or eight pieces of yarn 1″ long and glue these to the head, starting at the center of the head and running toward the face side. When the glue is dry, push the hair back over the head and glue down. Make a tightly coiled bun from one 3½″-long piece of yarn and glue this into place, concealing the first strands.

A girl doll may be dressed as follows: Make pantaloons from white material in the form of two tubes, with seams turned and hemmed. Slide these on the doll's legs and glue into place. Make the slip from white material as one larger tube, with seams turned and hemmed. Gather this around the waist and glue. Make a dress skirt from print material in the form of a large tube,

with seams turned and hemmed, and with ½″-wide lace sewed around the skirt bottom. Make the dress bodice from the same print material, with seams at the sides and under the sleeves being turned. One-fourth-inch-wide lace trim should be sewed inside the cuffs and down the front of the bodice. Place the bodice on the doll with the opening in the back. Gather the skirt around the waist. Hand-sew and glue the dress together. Tie and glue a ribbon around the waist, which will help conceal any raw edges. The dress should be about ⅛″ longer than the clothespin so that the doll can stand up by resting part of its weight on the dress. Bend the arms into elbows to make any desired gesture.

112

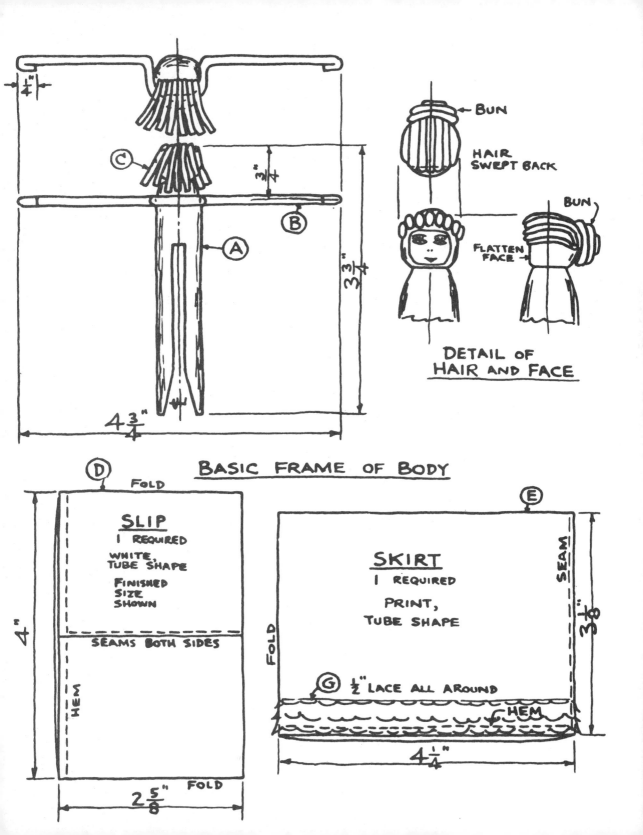

$\frac{1}{4}$"

C

B

A

$3\frac{3}{4}$"

$4\frac{3}{4}$"

BUN

HAIR
SWEPT BACK

BUN

FLATTEN
FACE

DETAIL OF
HAIR AND FACE

BASIC FRAME OF BODY

D

FOLD

SLIP
1 REQUIRED

WHITE,
TUBE SHAPE

FINISHED
SIZE
SHOWN

SEAMS BOTH SIDES

HEM

4"

FOLD

$2\frac{5}{8}$"

E

SKIRT
1 REQUIRED

PRINT,
TUBE SHAPE

FOLD

SEAM

$3\frac{3}{8}$"

G $\frac{1}{2}$" LACE ALL AROUND

HEM

$4\frac{1}{4}$"

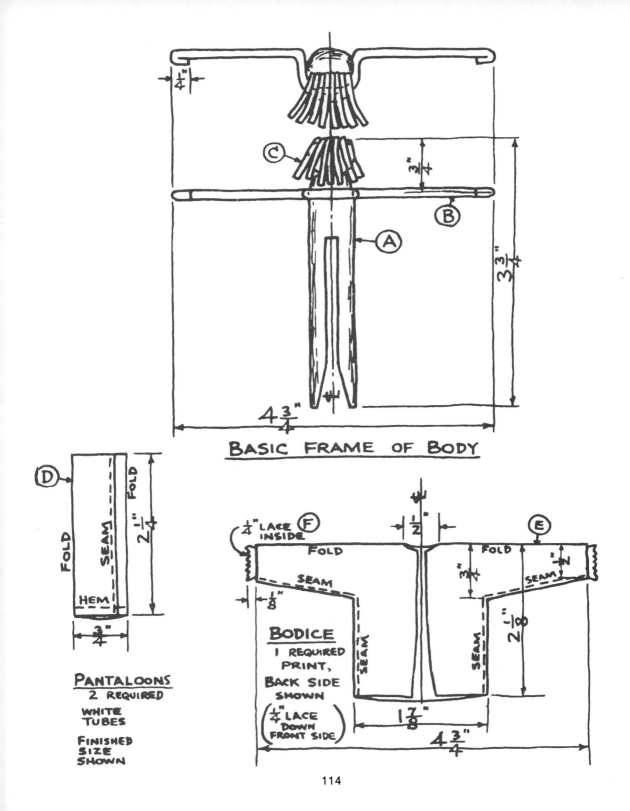

¼"

C

B

3"/4

A

3 3"/4

4 3"/4

BASIC FRAME OF BODY

D

FOLD

FOLD

SEAM

2 1"/4

HEM

3"/4

PANTALOONS
2 REQUIRED

WHITE
TUBES

FINISHED
SIZE
SHOWN

¼"LACE
INSIDE

F

FOLD

SEAM

1"/8

SEAM

BODICE
1 REQUIRED
PRINT,
BACK SIDE
SHOWN
(¼"LACE
DOWN
FRONT SIDE)

1 7"/8

½"

E

FOLD

2"/N

3"/4

SEAM

2 1"/8

4 3"/4

114

Additional material for boy doll
    PLASTIC WOOD (for feet)
    CLOTH, dark (pants)
    CLOTH, checkered or dotted (shirt and
    hatband)
    FELT, colored (hat and tie)

If the doll is to be dressed as a boy, the hair would be the same, except no bun is added. Dark-colored pants must be fashioned, and the shirt (which is the same pattern as for the girl's bodice) should be small-checkered or dotted material and without lace trim. A hat is made by rolling up and gluing a solid cylinder of felt, which in turn is glued onto a circular brim. A hatband matches the shirt material, and a felt necktie is glued on for contrast. Feet are molded from plastic wood, sanded level when dry, and painted. These enable the boy to stand up.

BOY

Hoop Snake

There is a legend often told by old-timers in mountainous regions. They claim to have seen a particular snake called the hoop snake, which, to make speed coming down a mountain, will take its tail in its mouth and roll down in hoop fashion. The old-timers will tell you with a straight face that they have found this snake driven through a tree like a straw in a tornado! Some say this snake can milk cows! Or is it a legend?

Anyway, our toy is only a harmless stuffed plaything. It is made of striped or spotted cotton cloth in the size and shape of a snake. It has slit eyes and a red forked tongue. If one believes in the hoop snake legend, a wooden spring clothespin may be sewed inside the mouth so that the snake can actually clamp onto its tail. The snake may also be tied into a vicious-looking knot.

MATERIALS

1 (A) UPPER BODY HALF, striped or spotted cloth 4″ x 46″
1 (B) LOWER BODY HALF, heavy bleached muslin 4″ x 46″
  (C) STUFFING, polyester fiber fill or cotton
  (D) THREAD, white cotton
2 (E) EYES, decorative elongated glass beads 5/16″ long
  (F) TONGUE, red felt scrap
  (G) CLOTHESPIN, spring type, wooden (optional)

Cut out the upper body half from a colorful striped or spotted snakelike cloth.

Cut out the lower body half from white bleached muslin, all dimensions being the same as for the upper half.

With the outside surfaces facing inside, sew the two halves together all around except for the 4″ section. Allow a seam margin of about 1/8″ around the edge. Turn the snake right side out through the 4″ gap.

Stuff the snake firmly by pushing the stuffing through the 4″ gap and working it down a little at a time. When full, close the gap by neatly hand-sewing. Sew on the red tongue and the two slit eyes.

If you want to let the hoop snake actually grab its tail with its mouth, it is possible to cut and sew a mouth into its head so that a spring-type clothespin may be sewn inside but not visible. Squeezing the head will open the mouth. The clothespin should be enclosed in a fitted muslin bag to prevent the stuffing from jamming the clothespin action.

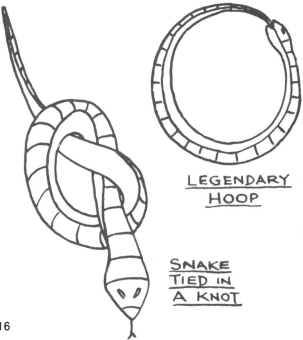

LEGENDARY HOOP

SNAKE TIED IN A KNOT

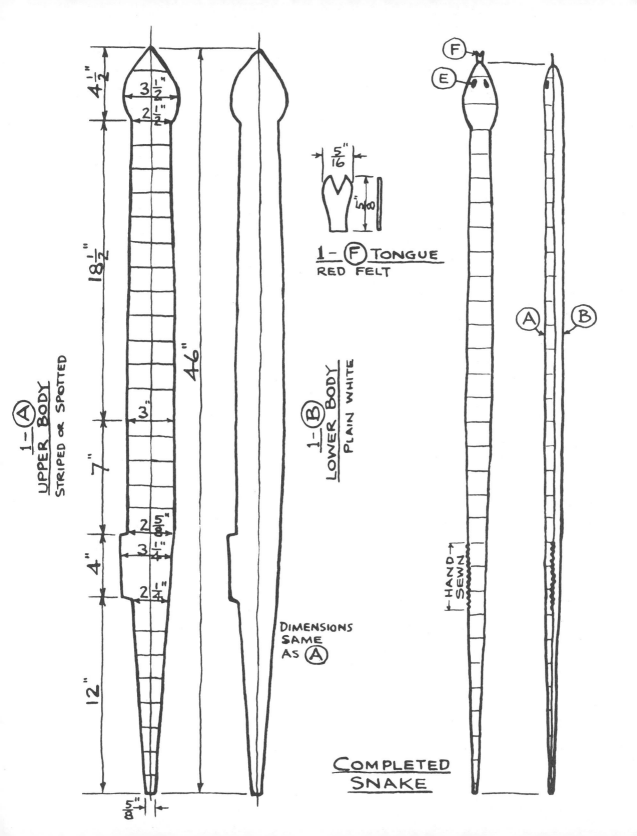

1 - Ⓐ
UPPER BODY
STRIPED OR SPOTTED

4½"

18½"

46"

7"

3"

4"

12"

5/8"

1 - Ⓑ
LOWER BODY
PLAIN WHITE

DIMENSIONS
SAME
AS Ⓐ

5/16"

3/8"

1 - Ⓕ TONGUE
RED FELT

HAND SEWN

Ⓕ Ⓔ

Ⓐ Ⓑ

COMPLETED
SNAKE

Doll Furniture

Miniature furniture is often used to heighten the realism of playing with dolls. Scaled to the size of the particular dolls used, it may include straight chairs, rocking chairs, doll beds complete with mattress and quilt, tables and chests. The construction may be of cardboard or, more substantially, of wood. Going further, complete dollhouses may be constructed to house the furniture and may consist of several rooms.

ROCKING CHAIR

1 (A) SEAT, wood 1/4" x 2 11/16" x 2 11/16" long

1 (B) BACK TOP, wood 1/4" x 5/8" x 2 7/8" long

2 (C) ROCKERS, wood 1/4" x 3/4" x 4 1/2" long

2 (D) ARMS, wood 1/4" x 3/16" x 2 1/2" long

4 (E) LEGS, birch dowels, 3/16" diam. x 1 1/4" long

1 (F) FRONT RUNG, birch dowel, 3/16" diam. x 1 15/16" long

2 (G) REAR UPRIGHTS, birch dowels, 3/16" diam. x 2 1/2" long

2 (H) FRONT UPRIGHTS, birch dowels, 3/16" diam. x 1" long

5 (I) BACK RUNGS, birch dowels, 1/8" diam. x 2 1/2" long

6 (J) ARM RUNGS, birch dowels, 1/8" diam. x 1" long

   (K) GLUE, white

ROCKING CHAIR

Cut all dowels to length, and cut out all the wooden pieces. The back top is curved and the seat is double-curved by filing with a half-round file and sanding. Drill holes about 1/8" deep to seat all dowels. Assemble all parts, using glue in the holes. The front rung between the legs is coped out to fit the legs, rather than being set into holes. Finish by sanding any rough spots.

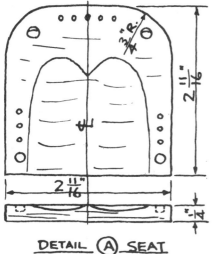

DETAIL Ⓐ SEAT
1 REQUIRED

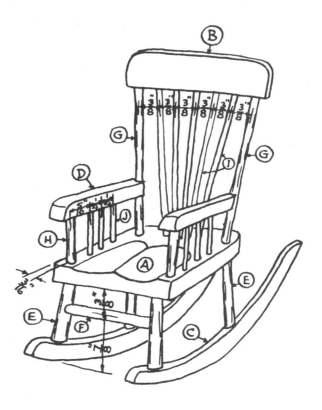

ROCKING CHAIR

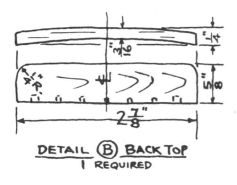

DETAIL Ⓑ BACK TOP
1 REQUIRED

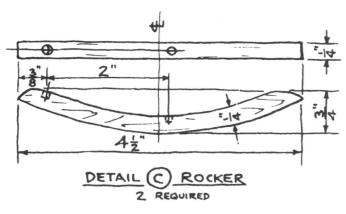

DETAIL Ⓒ ROCKER
2 REQUIRED

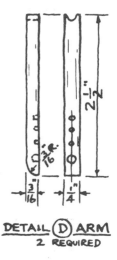

DETAIL Ⓓ ARM
2 REQUIRED

119

STRAIGHT CHAIR

2 (A) REAR LEGS, birch dowels, ¼″ diam. x 5¾″ long

2 (B) FRONT LEGS, birch dowels, ¼″ diam. x 2½″ long

6 (C) REAR AND SIDE RUNGS, birch dowels, ⅛″ diam. x 2″ long

2 (D) FRONT RUNGS, birch dowels, ⅛″ diam. x 2 5/16″ long

3 (E) LADDER RUNGS, wood ¼″ x 9/16″ x 2″ long

1 skein (F) RIBBON, Swistraw, honey beige, matte finish

(G) GLUE, white

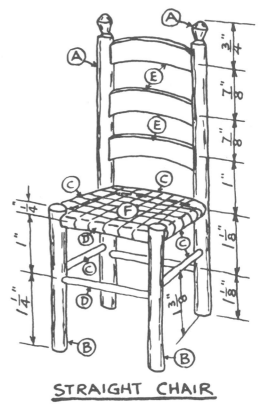

STRAIGHT CHAIR

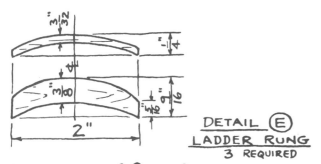

DETAIL (E)
LADDER RUNG
3 REQUIRED

STRAIGHT CHAIR

Cut all dowels to length; round ends of all the ¼″-diameter dowels by rotating lightly at an angle against a grinding wheel. The tops of the two back uprights are carved by hand to give an ornamental appearance. The ladder rungs are hand-carved to create a rounded shape. One-eighth-inch holes are drilled halfway into the legs in order to seat the rungs. Slots are made to seat the back ladder rungs by drilling two ⅛″ holes 3/16″ apart and then joining the two holes by carving the slot with a knife. The entire frame is assembled, using glue in the holes.

The honey-beige matte-finish Swistraw is a cellulose acetate ribbon which looks exactly like split oak when woven into the seat. The seat weaving is done in a conventional manner, wrapping the strips tightly across the frame in one direction, then weaving them through alternately in the other direction. The weaving is done dry, with the aid of a blunt darning needle. The ends of the ribbon are tucked in to conceal them.

BED

2 (A) HEADPOSTS, wood ½″ x ½″ x 4⅜″ long

2 (B) FOOTPOSTS, wood ½″ x ½″ x 3 9/16″ long

2 (C) TOP BOARDS, wood ¼″ x 13/16″ x 5⅛″ long

2 (D) BOTTOM BOARDS, wood ¼″ x ½″ x 5⅛″ long

4 (E) HEAD RUNGS, birch dowels ⅛″ diam. x 1¾″ long

4 (F) FOOT RUNGS, birch dowels ⅛″ diam. x ¾″ long

2 (G) RAILS, wood molding outside corner ¾″ x ½″ x 7¾″ long

1 (H) CORD, hard cotton 1/16″ diam. x 80″ long

16 (I) NAILS, box nails ⅞″ long

(J) GLUE, white

2 (K) MATTRESS COVER, cotton ticking 6¼″ x 8½″

1 (L) MATTRESS FILLER, blanket material 5¾″ x 7¾″

1 (M) QUILT FACE, cotton patchwork print 7⅝″ x 9⅝″

1 (N) QUILT BACKING, cotton percale, white 8½″ x 10½″

(O) THREAD, white

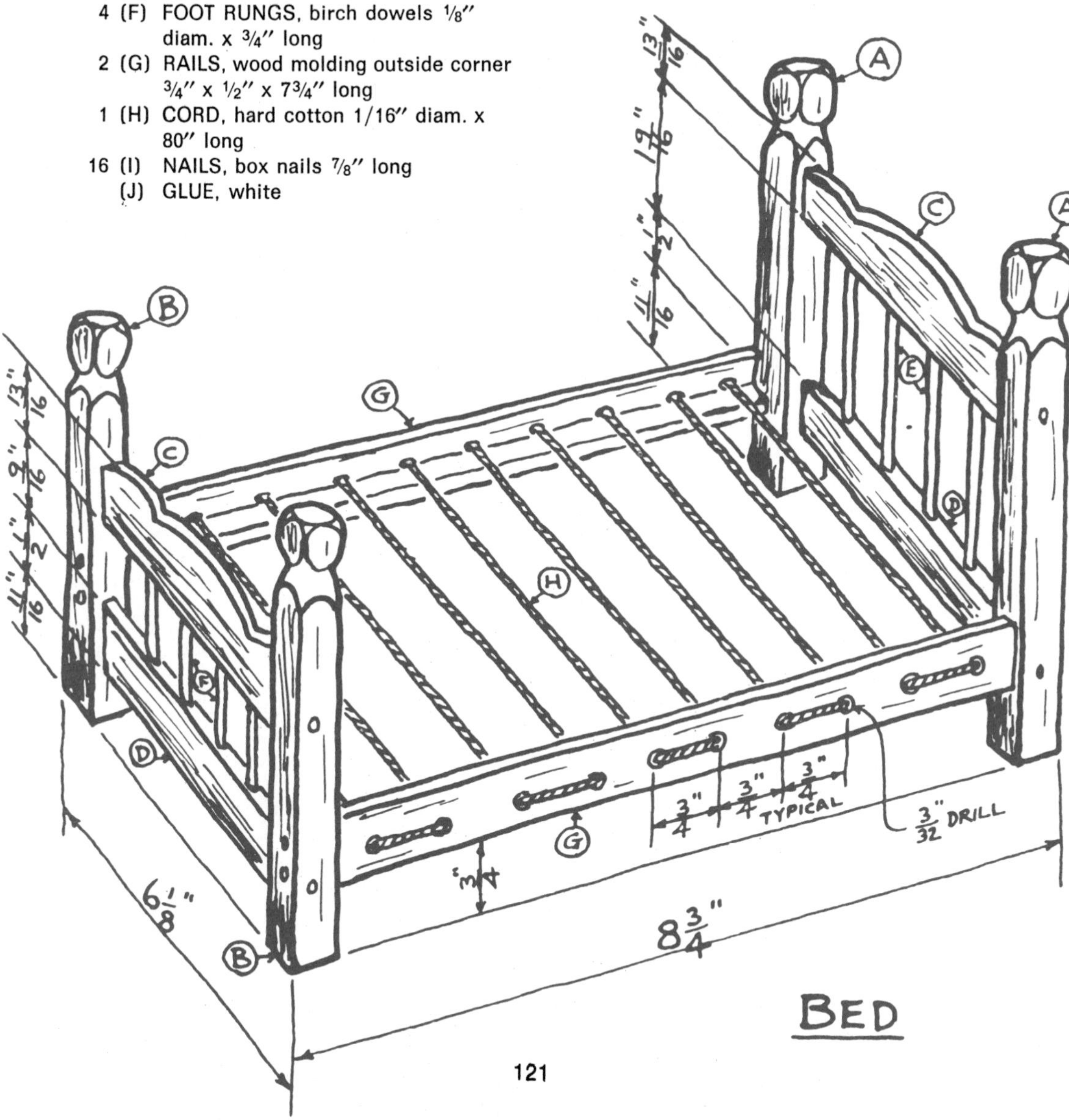

BED

121

BED

Cut all parts to size and shape. The bedposts look best if they are turned on a lathe, but they may be hand-carved or left plain. The headboards and the footboards are assembled first, being drilled for the vertical rungs, which are glued into place. Then the posts are glued and nailed on, using one nail per connection.

The side rails are drilled for the cord, then assembled to the headboard and footboard, using two nails per connection for extra strength. The cord is then laced back and forth through the holes in the rails, starting and ending with a knot.

The mattress cover is sewed on three sides, and the seams are turned. The mattress filler is inserted and the cover sewed up by hand. The quilt backing is sewed to the patchwork face, letting the white backing lap over the edge as a binding. Additional machine stitching may be done over the patchwork pattern to add realism.

Finger Puppets

It is possible to have an entire puppet theater in your hand by manipulating these tiny dolls on the tips of your fingers. There is an opening at the bottom of each doll which just fits the size of the fingers. The puppets may be made of knitted yarn or cloth, and often are colorfully decorated to caricature animals or people. The animals portrayed may be domestic, such as a dog, cat, pig, and chicken; or wild, such as a lion, elephant, frog, and skunk. The people characters may vary from a baby to an old lady. The puppets can be made in matched sets to illustrate nursery tales, such as "The Three Little Pigs," "Little Red Ridinghood," and "The Three Bears."

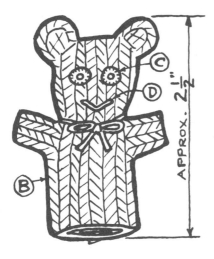

BEAR

for the head. Place a cotton ball in the head and cut yarn, leaving about a four- or five-inch length. Thread the needle with the piece of yarn and take stitches off onto yarn. Pull tight and pull yarn down through back of puppet and cut.

Ears

Pick up a stitch on back of the head on the right and make five double crochets in this stitch. Repeat on left side for the other ear.

Arms

Pick up one stitch about two stitches down from the neck and chain four. Make two single crochets in the first chain, and one single crochet in the next two chains.

Finishing

Sew on sequins for the eyes. Use red embroidery thread for the mouth.

Tie a bright contrasting piece of yarn around the neck for a bow.

Following are instructions for knitting two typical finger puppets, the bear and the frog:

BEAR

MATERIALS

3 (A) NEEDLES, No. 2 double-point
   (B) YARN, 4-ply wool, any color
2 (C) SEQUINS
   (D) THREAD, embroidery type, red

Body

Cast on twelve stitches. Divide, putting four stitches on each needle. Join and tie together, being careful not to twist. Knit until piece measures about 1 inch. On first needle, start decrease for neck as follows:

Knit 1, knit 2 stitches together, knit 1. Repeat on the following two needles. Should total nine stitches on the needles. Knit 1 round.

Head

Knit 1, increase in next stitch, knit 1. Repeat on following two needles. Should have twelve stitches back on the needles. Knit about five rows

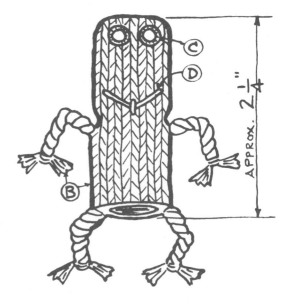

FROG

FROG

MATERIALS

3 (A) NEEDLES, No. 2 double-point
   (B) YARN, 4-ply wool, green
2 (C) SEQUINS
   (D) THREAD, embroidery type, colored

Body

Cast on twelve stitches. Divide, putting four stitches on each needle. Join and tie together, being careful not to twist. Knit until piece measures about one inch.

Neck

Knit 1, knit 2 stitches together, knit 1. Repeat on the following two needles. Should total nine stitches on the needles. Knit 1 round.

Head

Knit 1, increase in next stitch, knit 1. Repeat on the following two needles. Should have twelve stitches back on the needles. Knit about five rows for the head. Bind off. Place a cotton ball in the head. With a yarn needle, weave top of head together.

Arms

With a double piece of yarn, pick up a stitch on the right side of the body. Chain six stitches with a crochet hook and tie off, leaving a small amount of yarn to represent fingers. Repeat same for the left arm.

Legs

Similar to the arms, except done at the bottom of the puppet. Chain eight stitches instead of six as for the arms. Leave yarn to represent toes.

Finishing

Sew on sequins for the eyes. Double sequins are very effective, medium-size white ones sewed over large black ones. Make the mouth, using either yarn or embroidery thread, in a color contrasting with the green body.

The following is a list of some of the finger puppet characters which have been made:

Animals and Characters

Pigs
Frogs
Mice
Owls
Dogs
Cats
Hens
Chicks
Rabbits
Bears (three sizes)
Lions
Giraffes
Elephants
Devils
Octopuses
Humpty-Dumpty
Kangaroos
Pandas
Skunks
Alligators
Wolves
Cardinals
Bluebirds
Orioles
Snowmen
Snow Women

People

Grandpas
Grandmas
Men
Women
Boys
Girls
Babies
Brides
Bridegrooms
Little Red Ridinghood
Cowboys
Pirates
Hippies
Witches

Hand Puppets

These puppets are usually made of cloth and cover the entire hand like a glove. The center three fingers go into the head area, while the thumb and little finger give movement to the doll's arms. Figures may represent the traditional puppet characters like Punch and Judy, or they may portray other people or animals. Often the image is decidedly a caricature. Sets of hand puppets can be used to illustrate traditional children's stories. A small box can be built into a theatrical stage set, complete with a draw curtain. In this case, the operator's arms come up from below the stage so that he is not visible.

A basic pattern to fit hands up to adult size is diagrammed. Cut two sides from suitable heavy material, such as wide-wale corduroy, wool scraps, drapery material, and plush or bonded material. With the good sides turned in, sew the two sides together on a sewing machine, and hem around the bottom (wrist) area. When turned right side out, the seams will be concealed.

Now comes the imaginative part. By proper design, choice of decorative cloth and materials, the hand puppet can be made to look like a person: cowboy, Indian, policeman, railroad engineer, mountaineer, sunbonneted woman, boy, girl, doctor, farmer; or an animal character: dog, cat, bear, frog, sheep, elephant, bird. Several puppets can be made up as a set to suit familiar children's stories: Little Red Ridinghood, the wolf, and grandmother; The Three Bears; and The Three Little Pigs, for example.

People can have pink or brown cloth faces pieced in or appliquéd, with embroidered facial features and yarn hair. An Indian may have black braided hair tied with ribbons, colorful trim for a headband, and strung beads for a necklace. A girl or a woman may have a lace bodice and a ruffled skirt. Fantasy may permit pigs to wear overalls.

To use the hand puppet, merely insert your hand into it as if it were a glove, with the face toward your viewers. While telling the story illustrated by the puppet, wiggle your thumb and little finger for the hand action, and move your three center fingers to create head movements.

By modification of the head area, it is possible to build in a pocket area to make a wolf open its mouth and show its teeth, for example.

126

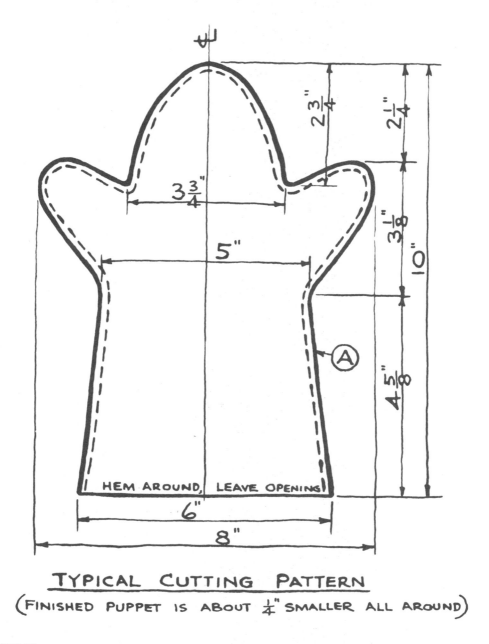

TYPICAL CUTTING PATTERN
(FINISHED PUPPET IS ABOUT ¼" SMALLER ALL AROUND)

MATERIALS

(A) CLOTH, heavy, firm but soft, for body
(B) THREAD, colors to suit
(C) CLOTH, colorful and decorative
(D) DECORATION, yarn, lace, ribbon, beads, felt, buttons, etc.

About the only design requirement for a hand puppet is that it should reasonably fit many hands, both those of children and adults. Beyond this, creativity can produce any kind of character from fantasy to reality.

127

Cornstalk Fiddle

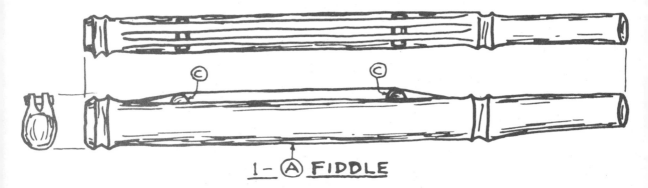

1- Ⓐ FIDDLE

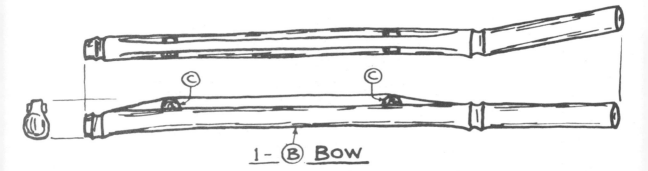

1- Ⓑ BOW

NOISEMAKERS

It's no Stradivarius, but this little stringed instrument can actually be played by a violinist, even though both the fiddle and the bow are made from a cornstalk. The stalk is a natural sounding board. A few strokes with a sharp knife will transform the ridges on the stalk into two strings with stops, and the bow is similarly made. The strings are rubbed with rosin, and you're ready to play. Even the music is corn!

MATERIALS

1 (A) FIDDLE, dry cornstalk 1½ joints, large
1 (B) BOW, dry cornstalk 1½ joints, medium
4 (C) STOPS, dry cornstalk ¾'' long, small diam.
1 (D) ROSIN, block
  (E) GLUE, white

Cut a cornstalk in the fall, when the stalk is mature and dry. The fiddle is made from a length of 1½ joints taken from near the base end of the stalk, where it is larger. At this end, each joint has a natural deep groove between two ridges. A stroke with a knife or razor blade will separate the two ridges from the stalk but leave them attached at the joints. Two half-round sections from the stalk top are cut, forced in and glued to become bridge stops. The ridges are now strings, and the stalk is the sounding board.

The bow is made from a length of 1½ joints taken from a point midway on the stalk. Here the immature stalk does not have the deep grooving. With a knife or razor blade, separate a single string from the stalk while leaving the ends attached at the joints. Again, two half-round sections from the stalk top are cut, forced in and glued, completing the bow.

Rosin is rubbed on the strings of both the bow and the fiddle. It is played in a conventional manner, including fingering to vary the pitch.

IN USE

Bull-Roarer

This toy makes a reversing roaring noise, much like an angry, snorting bull. It has aerodynamic properties that make it quite a novelty even today.

The noise is created by grasping the handle and swinging the flat wooden paddle at the end of the string around your head continuously in one direction. The paddle will wind up the string until it is tight in one direction, whereupon it will reverse and unwind, only to rewind in the opposite direction. Again and again it will reverse, making surprisingly loud noises as it accelerates and decelerates at each reversal. Always use great caution to avoid striking people or objects.

The bull-roarer has been known to various peoples all over the world, including the American Indians. Even today certain tribes in South America use a large version for driving fish up narrow streams, while others use it to warn women away from all-male mystical rituals.

MATERIALS

1 (A) PADDLE, birch plywood ¼″ x 1 9/16″ x 11⅝″, two good sides
1 (B) HANDLE, hardwood branch ⅝″ diam. x 9″ long
1 (C) SWIVEL, galvanized steel wire, #16 ga. x 5⅝″ long
1 (D) CORD, #21 nylon twine, 185-pound test, 42″ long

Cut out the paddle. Sand all edges smooth to the touch, but do not overdo the sanding, as round edges can reduce the noisemaking capability of the paddle. Drill the ⅛″-diameter hole in the paddle.

Cut the handle to length. Grind a groove into the handle for the swivel, by rotating the handle against a running ½″-wide grinding wheel stone with a radiused edge. Be sure to use a safety shield, wear safety glasses, and be careful when performing this operation, as grinding of wood can be dangerous. Make the groove smooth and a true circle for good operation. A second groove is sometimes added for ornamentation.

The swivel is made by cutting stiff wire to length, crimping and bending, and wrapping and shaping it around the groove of the handle. Check to assure that the swivel has a loose fit with no binding but is in no danger of coming off.

Cut the nylon cord to 42″ length. Prevent the cut ends of cord from fraying by fusing (melting) them over a match or candle flame. Tie one end of the cord through the hole in the paddle and the other end to the swivel, using a bowline knot for each. This knot is less likely to slip than any other knot; still it must be tied tightly, with about ¾″ of excess cord left beyond the knot.

Be careful in swinging the bull-roarer so that you do not endanger anyone nearby.

BULL-ROARER IN USE

ASSEMBLY

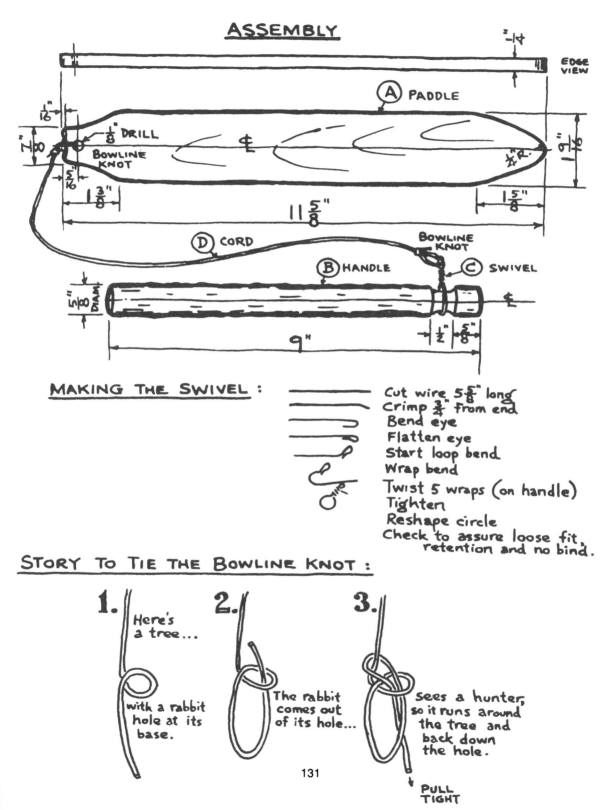

EDGE VIEW

$\frac{2}{-14}$

(A) PADDLE

$\frac{1}{16}"$

$\frac{1}{8}"$ DRILL

$2\frac{1}{00}"$

BOWLINE KNOT

$\frac{5}{16}"$

$1\frac{3}{8}"$

$11\frac{5}{8}"$

$\frac{1}{4}"$ R.

$1\frac{9}{16}"$

$1\frac{5}{8}"$

(D) CORD

BOWLINE KNOT

(B) HANDLE

(C) SWIVEL

$\frac{5}{00}"$ DIAM

9"

$\frac{1}{2}"$

$\frac{5}{8}"$

MAKING THE SWIVEL:

Cut wire $5\frac{5}{8}"$ long
Crimp $\frac{3}{4}"$ from end
Bend eye
Flatten eye
Start loop bend
Wrap bend
Twist 5 wraps (on handle)
Tighten
Reshape circle
Check to assure loose fit,
    retention and no bind.

STORY TO TIE THE BOWLINE KNOT:

1. Here's a tree... with a rabbit hole at its base.

2. The rabbit comes out of its hole...

3. sees a hunter, so it runs around the tree and back down the hole.

PULL TIGHT

Whistles

The most common whistle is made from a short section of a willow branch, best when cut in the spring. The bark may be lightly hammered to bruise it a little, then the center can be pushed out of the bark. The center is carved out to the interior shape of a whistle air passage, while the bark is notched to become the vibrating reed. When the center is slipped back into its original position in the bark jacket, you have a whistle.

Other whistles can be made of hollow elder branches or solid wood which is bored out. A slide whistle with a variable-pitch sound may be made from a longer piece of willow branch by moving the end plug in and out while blowing. The varying-size whistle chamber causes changes in pitch and harmonics.

Another whistle uses a blade of grass or a laurel leaf as a reed to produce a shrill sound. A piece of wood is split; then a space is carved in for the tightly stretched reed. It is held in place by wrapping the split wood back together with rubber bands.

A neck cord may be added for convenience by drilling a hole through the nonfunctional end of the whistle body, and threading through and tying the cord.

Test the whistle by blowing. Some adjustment or sharpening of the "reed" with a pocketknife may be needed.

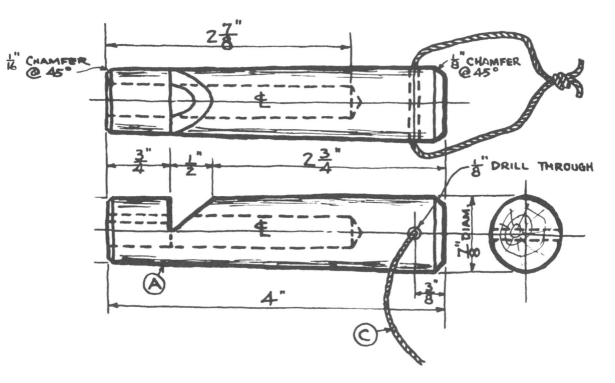

ASSEMBLY

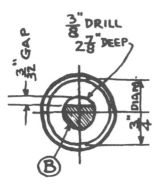

MATERIALS

1 (A) BODY, hardwood ⁷⁄₈″ diam. x 4″ long
1 (B) PLUG, birch dowel ³⁄₈″ diam. x ¾″ long
1 (C) NECK CORD, nylon or cotton braid 3/32″
      diam. x 30″ long

The whistle shown is to be hand-turned on
a lathe and has the small-diameter end at the
mouthpiece. Other designs have the large diameter at the mouthpiece, are of true cylindrical
shape, have a square cross section, or are totally
unfinished on the outside. Actually, it is the
inside geometry and finish that count.

Cut the whistle body to size (longer for
chucking, if turned on a lathe), and shape the
outside. Bore the inside to the depth shown and
cut the notch which provides the vibrating "reed"
of the whistle. Cut the plug to length, cut away
a segment of the top edge of the plug, and firmly
insert it in the bore.

Turkey Call

Obviously, a turkey call is made for use in attracting the wild turkey while hunting. However, it is included here as a folk toy because the call has probably been used more in playing than in hunting. It is a small wooden box having a loosely hinged, rounded cover with a handle. The cover is coated with chalk. When the cover is scraped across the edges of the sounding box, it makes a sound very much like the "gobble" of a turkey. With a little practice, even a turkey can be fooled.

Another version of the call is made of a dished circular piece of wood with a small box nail in the center. It is held in the palm of the hand while the nail head is drawn across a scythe-sharpening stone. The sound is pure turkey talk.

MATERIALS

1 (A) BODY, wood 1⅜" x 1⅞" x 7⅛"
2 (B) SIDES, hardwood 3/32" x 1⅞" x 7⅛"
1 (C) COVER, hardwood ¼" x 1½" x 8⅜"
1 (D) CHALKBOARD, hardwood ¼" x ½" x 1½"
1 (E) ROOFING NAIL, 1¼" long
1 (F) RUBBER TUBING, 5/16" OD x 3/16" ID x ⅛"
       long
    (G) GLUE, white
    (H) CHALK

Lay out all wooden parts. Two 1"-diameter holes may be bored through the body if desired to make the sawing job easier. Make a starting hole for the roofing nail, and punch the depression indicated (concentric with the nail hole). The purpose of the depression is to retain the piece of rubber tubing. Cut out the two thin sides and glue them to the body. When the glue has set, round the ends of the box by sawing and sanding.

Cut out the cover and drill the nail hole. Cut out the chalkboard, shape and smooth it, and glue it to the underside of the cover. Attach the cover to the body by driving in the roofing nail, but with the short piece of rubber tubing in between as a flexible washer.

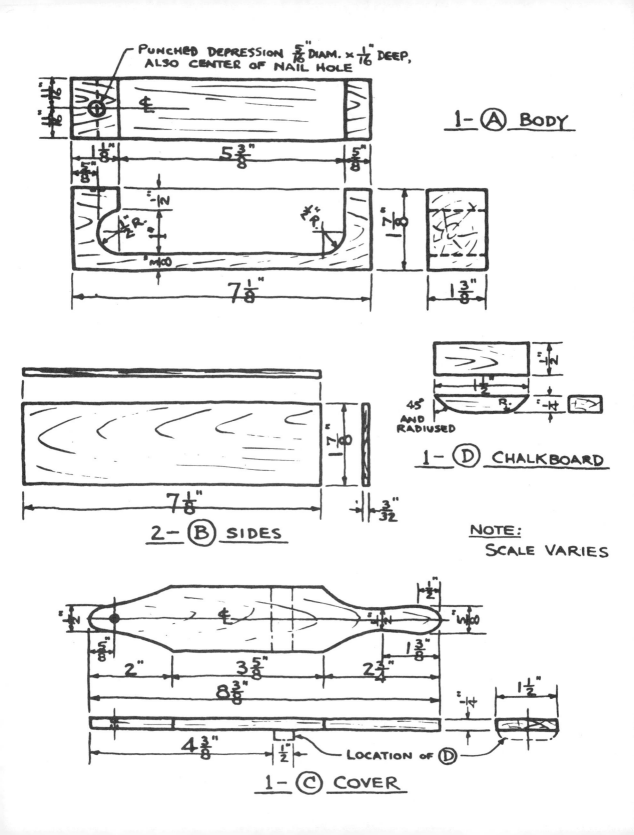

PUNCHED DEPRESSION $\frac{5}{16}$" DIAM. × $\frac{1}{16}$" DEEP, ALSO CENTER OF NAIL HOLE

1- Ⓐ BODY

$\frac{9}{16}$"
$\frac{9}{16}$"

¢

$1\frac{1}{8}$" $5\frac{3}{8}$" $\frac{5}{8}$"

$\frac{5}{8}$"

$\frac{1}{2}$"R.

$2\frac{1}{2}$"

$\frac{1}{2}$"R.

$1\frac{7}{8}$"

$2\frac{3}{8}$"

$7\frac{1}{8}$"

$1\frac{3}{8}$"

2- Ⓑ SIDES

$1\frac{7}{8}$"

$7\frac{1}{8}$"

$\frac{3}{32}$"

1 - Ⓓ CHALKBOARD

$\frac{1}{2}$"

$1\frac{1}{2}$"

45° AND RADIUSED

R.

$\frac{1}{4}$"

NOTE:
SCALE VARIES

1- Ⓒ COVER

$\frac{1}{2}$"

$\frac{1}{2}$"

¢

$\frac{5}{8}$"

$1\frac{3}{8}$"

$1\frac{3}{4}$"

2" $3\frac{5}{8}$" $2\frac{3}{4}$"

$8\frac{3}{8}$"

$\frac{1}{4}$"

$1\frac{1}{2}$"

$4\frac{3}{8}$" $\frac{1}{2}$"   LOCATION OF Ⓓ

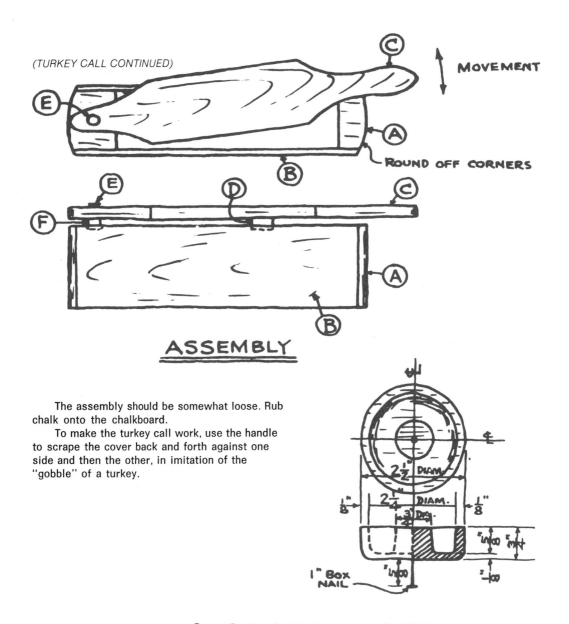

MOVEMENT

ROUND OFF CORNERS

ASSEMBLY

The assembly should be somewhat loose. Rub chalk onto the chalkboard.

To make the turkey call work, use the handle to scrape the cover back and forth against one side and then the other, in imitation of the "gobble" of a turkey.

$2\frac{1}{2}$" DIAM.

$2\frac{1}{4}$" DIAM.

$\frac{1}{8}$"

$\frac{1}{8}$"

$\frac{3}{4}$" Dia.

1" BOX NAIL

SIMPLE ALTERNATE DESIGN

— HAND-CARVED OR TURNED ON A LATHE, NAIL DRIVEN IN.

— RUB THE NAIL HEAD ON A WHETSTONE OR A ROUGH SANDSTONE PEBBLE.

— SOUNDS SURPRISINGLY LIKE THE OTHER TURKEY CALL.

Harmonica

A melody can be played on this little instrument, simple as it is. The harmonica is a pair of slightly carved-out stretcher sticks bound together at the ends by small rubber bands and using for a reed a large rubber band or a large blade of grass. To play the harmonica, blow between the sticks to produce a tone and vary the tone frequency by squeezing the sticks. A little practice will produce "music?"

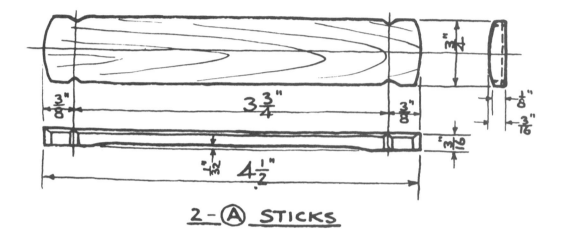

2-Ⓐ STICKS

MATERIALS

2 (A) STICKS, wood 3/16″ x 3/4″ x 4½″
2 (B) RUBBER BANDS, small, 2½″ long
1 (C) RUBBER BAND, large, ¼″ wide x 2½″ long

Cut out the two sticks. Carve a 1/32″ recess in each so that the two sticks will be about 1/16″ apart when placed together. Carve notches near the ends, round the pieces, and sand them so that they are smooth. Place the two sticks together with the large rubber band between them. Fasten by wrapping the small rubber bands around the ends. Test the harmonica by blowing between the sticks while squeezing them to vary the tone.

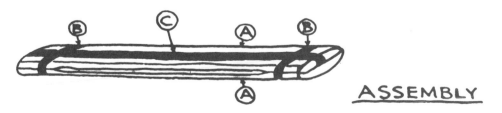

ASSEMBLY

137

Crow Call

The normal function of a crow call is to attract crows while hunting. It is included here, however, because children have fun playing with it. It is a reed-type horn which, when blown, makes a guttural "caw" sound. The vibrating element may be a celluloid or plastic collar stay or similar sheet material.

In trying to attract crows, stay hidden and quiet, and muffle the sound of the call by cupping your hand over the outlet. Crows are intelligent and curious but have very sensitive vision and hearing. They may return after a gunshot, if they have not actually seen the caller.

MATERIALS

1 (A) BARREL, hardwood 1⅛" diam. x 3½" long
2 (B) JAWS, birch dowel ½" diam. x 2½" long
1 (C) REED, celluloid or plastic 2⅜" x ½" x .012" thick

The barrel may be a smooth wood turning, or it may be made from a rough, but dry branch of a tree. Bore the 15/32" hole through the body and smooth the ends.

The jaws, which hold the reed, are made from a piece of ½"-diameter dowel. Drill the 15/64" hole 2⅛" deep on the center line of the dowel. Carefully split the dowel in half by sawing with a narrow blade. Notch the V clearance, round the ends, and carve the teeth grips.

For the reed, a plastic collar stay may be used. The reed shown, however, is shaped to give a better tonal quality to the call. It may be made of plastic about .012" thick such as is sometimes used for page protectors and wallet-size calendars.

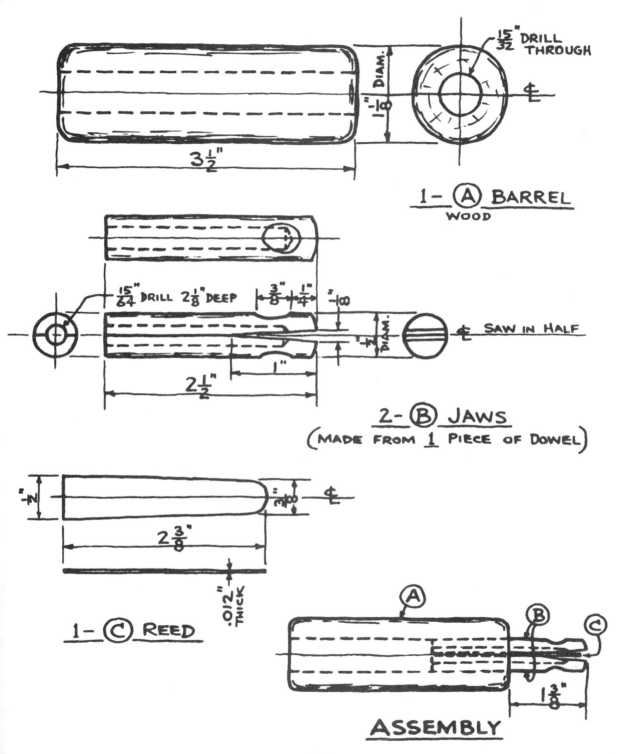

$\frac{15}{32}''$ DRILL THROUGH

Diam.

$1\frac{1}{8}''$

₵

$3\frac{1}{2}''$

1 – Ⓐ BARREL
WOOD

$\frac{15}{64}''$ DRILL $2\frac{1}{8}''$ DEEP

$\frac{3}{8}''$ $\frac{1}{4}''$

$1\frac{1}{8}''$

Diam.

$\frac{1}{2}''$

₵ SAW IN HALF

$2\frac{1}{2}''$

$1''$

2 – Ⓑ JAWS
(MADE FROM 1 PIECE OF DOWEL)

$\frac{1}{2}''$

$\frac{3}{8}''$

₵

$2\frac{3}{8}''$

.012" THICK

1 – Ⓒ REED

Ⓐ   Ⓑ   Ⓒ

$1\frac{3}{8}''$

ASSEMBLY

Ticktack

This device resembles the spool tractor but has a different use. It is made from a wooden spool with notches in the rims, a spindle stick, another stick for a handle, and a string. The string is wound around the spool as if it were a top.

The purpose is to scare people, especially around Halloween time. The ticktack is placed against the outside of the windowpane, and when the string is pulled, the notched spool makes a terrifying racket on the window glass but without harming it.

MATERIALS

1 (A) SPOOL, wood 2¼″ diam. x 2⅞″ long
1 (B) HANDLE, wood 7″ x 1″ x ¾″
1 (C) SPINDLE, birch dowel ⅜″ diam. x 4½″ long
1 (D) WASHER, wood ¾″ diam. x ¼″ long
1 (E) CAP, wood ¾″ diam. x ⅝″ long
1 (F) CORD, #21 nylon twine or cotton 48″ long
1 (G) TAB, birch dowel ⅜″ diam. x ½″ long
   (H) GLUE, white

A large commercial wooden thread spool may be used. However, shown here is a hand-turned wooden spool made on a lathe. Bore out the center hole, and carve or rout the deep notches in the rims of the spool. Cut all the other wooden parts to size; drill the handle, washer, cap, and tab. File and sand the handle until it is smooth to the touch. Glue the spindle into the hole in the handle. Assemble the parts, making sure that the spool is loose and free to spin. Cut the cord to length; thread on the tab; tie a knot in each end of the cord and an additional knot to secure the tab at one end.

To work the ticktack, wind the cord around the spool, leaving the tab on the outside. Holding the handle, place the spool against a windowpane. With the free hand, pull the cord. Then run, because you will have created a terrible racket!

140

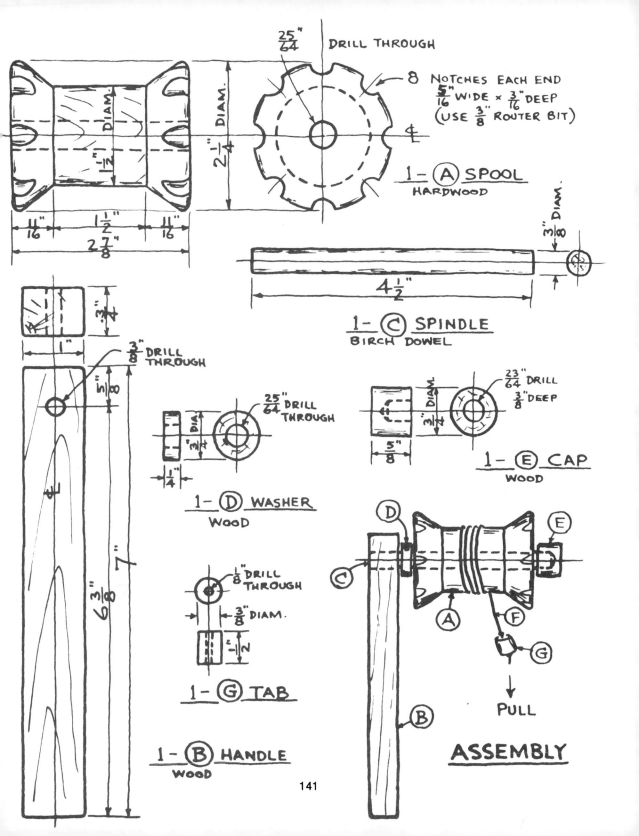

$\frac{25}{64}$" DRILL THROUGH

8 NOTCHES EACH END
$\frac{5}{16}$" WIDE × $\frac{3}{16}$" DEEP
(USE $\frac{3}{8}$" ROUTER BIT)

DIAM.

DIAM.

$2\frac{1}{4}$" DIAM.

$1\frac{1}{2}$"

$\frac{11}{16}$" $1\frac{1}{2}$" $\frac{11}{16}$"
$2\frac{7}{8}$"

1 – (A) SPOOL
HARDWOOD

$\frac{3}{8}$" DIAM.

$4\frac{1}{2}$"

1 – (C) SPINDLE
BIRCH DOWEL

$\frac{3}{4}$"

1"

$\frac{3}{8}$" DRILL THROUGH

$\frac{5}{8}$"

$6\frac{3}{8}$"   7"

$\frac{25}{64}$" DRILL THROUGH

DIA.

$\frac{3}{4}$"

$\frac{1}{4}$"

1 – (D) WASHER
WOOD

$\frac{23}{64}$" DRILL
$\frac{3}{8}$" DEEP

DIAM.

$\frac{3}{4}$"

$\frac{5}{8}$"

1 – (E) CAP
WOOD

$\frac{1}{8}$" DRILL THROUGH

$\frac{3}{8}$" DIAM.

$\frac{1}{2}$"

1 – (G) TAB

1 – (B) HANDLE
WOOD

D
C
A
B
E
F
G

PULL

ASSEMBLY

Rattletrap

(OR HORSE FIDDLE)

This noisemaker was popular at Halloween time and at shivarees (charivaris). It has a handle with a star-shaped cam. Swinging loosely around the cam is a frame holding a thin wooden spring leaf. As the frame is swung around, the spring leaf clacks against the star cam, making a terrible racket.

MATERIALS

1 (A) BODY, wood 1⅝″ x 2¼″ x 7⅛″
1 (B) COG, hardwood ¾″ x 1½″ x 1½″
1 (C) SHAFT, birch dowel ⅜″ diam. x 3½″ long
1 (D) HANDLE, wooden branch ¾″ diam. x 5″ long
1 (E) CAP, wooden branch ¾″ diam. x ¾″ long
1 (F) PIN, birch dowel ⅛″ diam. x 1″ long
1 (G) PAWL, hardwood ⅛″ x 1″ x 4¾″
6 (H) NAILS, finishing nails 1½″ long
  (I) GLUE, white

on the handle and cap and drilling and installing the retaining pin. Finally, install the pawl while testing the action, and when satisfactory, drive nails through the body and pawl.

To use, grasp the handle and swing the body portion around, causing the cog and pawl to create noise.

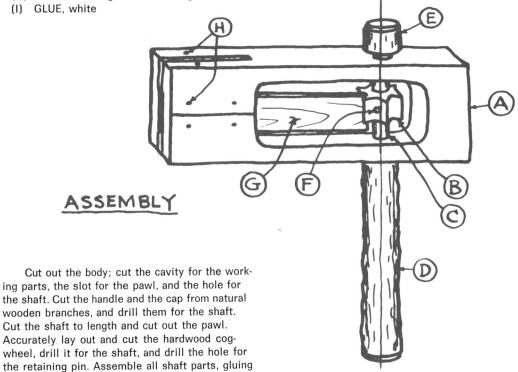

ASSEMBLY

Cut out the body; cut the cavity for the working parts, the slot for the pawl, and the hole for the shaft. Cut the handle and the cap from natural wooden branches, and drill them for the shaft. Cut the shaft to length and cut out the pawl. Accurately lay out and cut the hardwood cog-wheel, drill it for the shaft, and drill the hole for the retaining pin. Assemble all shaft parts, gluing

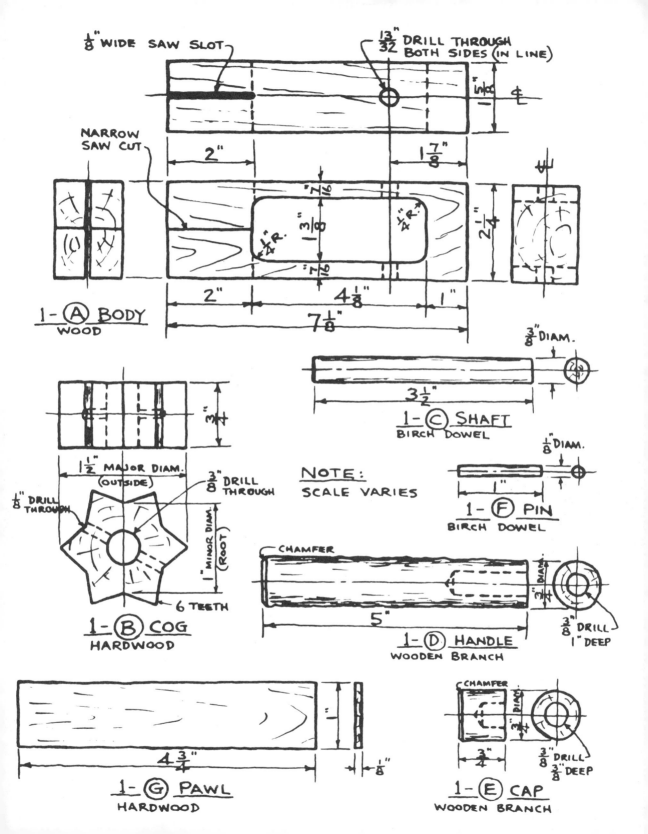

$\frac{1}{8}$" WIDE SAW SLOT

$\frac{13}{32}$" DRILL THROUGH BOTH SIDES (IN LINE)

NARROW SAW CUT

2"

$1\frac{7}{8}$"

$\frac{7}{16}$"

$\frac{3}{8}$"

$\frac{7}{16}$"

$\frac{1}{4}$ R.

$\frac{1}{4}$ R.

$2\frac{1}{4}$"

2"

$4\frac{1}{8}$"

1"

$7\frac{1}{8}$"

1- Ⓐ BODY
WOOD

$\frac{3}{8}$" DIAM.

$3\frac{1}{2}$"

1- Ⓒ SHAFT
BIRCH DOWEL

$\frac{1}{2}$" MAJOR DIAM.
(OUTSIDE)

$\frac{3}{8}$" DRILL THROUGH

$\frac{1}{8}$" DRILL THROUGH

1" MINOR DIAM. (ROOT)

6 TEETH

1- Ⓑ COG
HARDWOOD

NOTE:
SCALE VARIES

$\frac{1}{8}$" DIAM.

1"

1- Ⓕ PIN
BIRCH DOWEL

CHAMFER

$\frac{3}{4}$" DIAM.

5"

$\frac{3}{8}$" DRILL 1" DEEP

1- Ⓓ HANDLE
WOODEN BRANCH

$4\frac{3}{4}$"

$\frac{1}{8}$"

1- Ⓖ PAWL
HARDWOOD

CHAMFER

$\frac{3}{4}$"

$\frac{3}{8}$" DRILL $\frac{3}{8}$" DEEP

1- Ⓔ CAP
WOODEN BRANCH

Snapping Turtle

This one is a play on words. The shape is that of a cloth turtle. But sewed inside is the dome lid of a wide-mouth jar used in food canning. When pressed with the fingers, the lid will snap in oil can fashion, and so we have a snapping turtle.

Another oil-can type was the cricket, made from a piece of flat-strip spring steel bent into a V shape and slightly dished with a hammer. It would make a snapping sound whenever the V was squeezed or released.

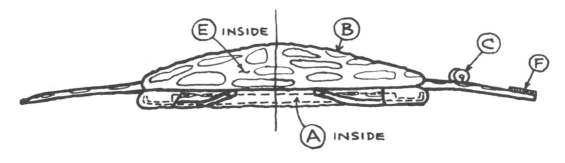

MATERIALS

1 (A) WIDE-MOUTH DOME LID, for canning jar
1 (B) CLOTH, heavy cotton, 6″ x 12″
2 (C) EYES, glass beads, approximately ⅛″ diam.
  (D) THREAD, color to match cloth
  (E) STUFFING, cotton or polyester fiber
  (F) CLOTH, red

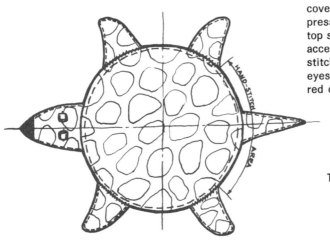

The noisemaker is a wide-mouth dome lid about 3 5/16″ in diameter. Two circles of cloth are cut out and sewed together, wrong side out, about ¾ of the way around to fit the lid. The legs, head and tail are made from scrap and sewed into the body cover. The cover is turned right side out to conceal all seams.

The lid is inserted upside down into the cover so it will make a snapping noise when pressed from below. Stuffing is added only on the top side to represent the turtle's back. Then the access hole in the cover is closed by hand stitching. Two small glass beads are sewed on as eyes, and a mouth is made of a small scrap of red cloth.

To make the turtle snap, just squeeze it.

WOODCARVER'S SPECIALTIES

Peach Seed Monkey

This traditional carving exercise is the peach seed monkey, an intricate design carved in the hard, corrugated wood of a peach stone. The shape of the monkey conforms somewhat to the natural form of the peach seed.

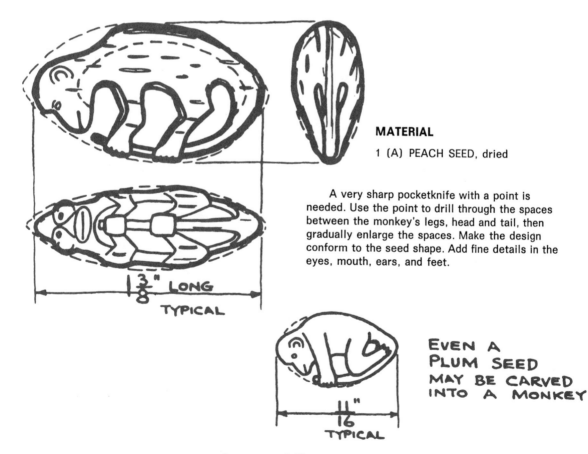

MATERIAL

1 (A) PEACH SEED, dried

A very sharp pocketknife with a point is needed. Use the point to drill through the spaces between the monkey's legs, head and tail, then gradually enlarge the spaces. Make the design conform to the seed shape. Add fine details in the eyes, mouth, ears, and feet.

1 3/8" LONG TYPICAL

11/16" TYPICAL

EVEN A PLUM SEED MAY BE CARVED INTO A MONKEY

The Tree

VARIATION

MATERIAL

1 (A) STICK, straight-grained wood, ½" diameter
x 12" long

Little can be said about the making of this
one except that it requires a proper piece of wood,
a sharp knife, a steady hand, a delicate touch,
and a creative imagination. That's about all there
is to wood carving.

GLUE INTO
ANOTHER
PIECE OF
WOOD FOR
A BASE

This project is a traditional test of the carver's sharp knife and his
steady hand; but properly done, the end product is a very attractive decoration resembling an evergreen tree.

The whittler starts with a straight-grained wooden stick about ½" diameter after removal of the bark. He whittles down the end of the stick but
is careful to leave all the shavings connected to the stick at the end of
the cut. This makes the topmost spread of branches. Then he drops down
and starts shaving up the next spread, leaving the shavings connected. Then
he drops down again to make the next spread of branches. Any number of
branches can be carved. The tree may be mounted in a hole drilled in a
heavier piece of wood so that it can stand up.

VEHICLES AND FLYING TOYS

Spool Tractor

This is an early-day power toy remembered by many people today. It is made from a wooden spool, a rubber band, and a stick. When the assembly is wound up and placed on the floor, it becomes a self-powered vehicle and will travel quite a distance. The rims of the spool may be notched for traction, and a washer made from a piece of soap may be used as a lubricant on the stick side.

MATERIALS

1 (A) SPOOL, wood 2½″ diam. x 2⅞″ long
1 (B) STICK, wooden branch ⅜″ diam. x 5″ long
1 (C) RETAINER, wooden branch ¼″ diam. x ⅞″ long
1 (D) WASHER, birch dowel ¾″ diam. x 3/16″ long
1 (E) RUBBER BAND, ¼″ wide x 2½″ long

A large commercial wooden thread spool may be used. However, as these are becoming increasingly difficult to obtain, dimensions are given here for the hand turning of a wooden spool on a lathe. Bore the center hole, carve the notches in the "wheels," and carve the shallow groove in one end to hold the retainer. Cut and carve the retainer and the stick. Cut the washer. Assemble the tractor by looping the rubber band around the stick and through the washer, then pulling the rubber band through the spool with a wire hook and anchoring it around the retainer in its groove.

Test the tractor by winding it up and letting it run on the floor. A little wax or soap applied between the washer and the spool may make it operate better.

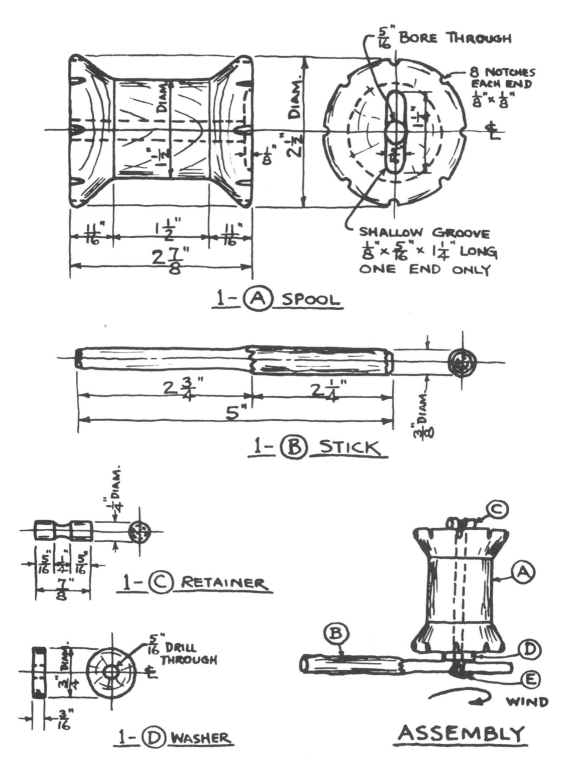

$\frac{5}{16}"$ BORE THROUGH

8 NOTCHES EACH END $\frac{1}{8}" \times \frac{1}{8}"$

SHALLOW GROOVE $\frac{1}{8}" \times \frac{5}{16}" \times 1\frac{1}{4}"$ LONG ONE END ONLY

$2\frac{3}{8}"$ DIAM.

$\frac{11}{16}"$ $1\frac{1}{2}"$ $\frac{11}{16}"$

$2\frac{7}{8}"$

1 - Ⓐ SPOOL

$2\frac{3}{4}"$ $2\frac{1}{4}"$

5"

$\frac{3}{8}"$ DIAM.

1 - Ⓑ STICK

$\frac{1}{4}"$ DIAM.

$\frac{5}{16}"$ $\frac{1}{4}"$ $\frac{5}{16}"$

$\frac{7}{8}"$

1 - Ⓒ RETAINER

$\frac{5}{16}"$ DRILL THROUGH

$\frac{3}{4}"$ DIAM.

$\frac{3}{16}"$

1 - Ⓓ WASHER

WIND

ASSEMBLY

149

Paddle Wheel Boat

Most of the male adults in the United States today built rubber-band-powered boats when they were boys. For some reason, however, their sons just do not do this kind of thing. The boat usually is a simple flat board, pointed at the bow end and with an open cutout for the paddle wheel at the stern. More pretentious models may have a superstructure and smokestacks. The paddle wheel consists of two small flat boards notched and fitted together in egg-crate construction, which provides four blades for the wheel. A rubber band of suitable size is the power. When the wheel is wound up by hand and the boat placed in the water, the craft will move ahead. Two or more boats can be raced.

Other kinds of simple-operating boats can be made, including sailboats, screw propeller types, and even diving submarines.

MATERIALS

1 (A) HULL, white pine ¾" x 2⅝" x 8¼"
1 (B) CABIN, white pine ¾" x 1¾" x 3½"
2 (C) STACKS, birch dowels ⅜" diam. x 1¾" long
2 (D) PADDLES, white pine ⅛" x 1⅛" x 2¼"
1 (E) RUBBER BAND, approx. 1¾" length (test other lengths)
  (F) GLUE, *waterproof*
  (G) SHOE POLISH, *waterproof* liquid black

Cut out the hull and wheelhouse (cabin) from ¾"-thick white pine. Shape the bow and stern; cut notches in the stern to hold the rubber band. Drill the wheelhouse for the stacks made of birch dowels. Use waterproof glue to fasten the wheelhouse to the hull, the stacks to the wheelhouse, and also to fasten the two halves of the lap-jointed paddle wheel. No finish is needed on the boat, but the stacks can be made more interesting by painting them with waterproof black shoe polish. Place the small rubber band in the notches and across the wheel well. Insert the paddle wheel in the rubber band and wind it up. When placed in water, the boat will travel under its own power.

Spare rubber bands can be carried around the two stacks. A name can be painted on the two sides of the cabin, such as the *Robert E. Lee* or the *Delta Queen.*

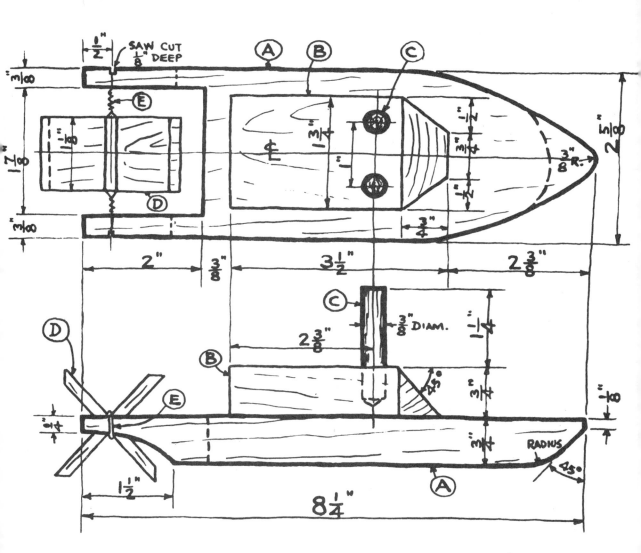

SAW CUT 1/8" DEEP

1/2"

3/16"

17/8"

3/16"

E

D

A B C

3/4" 3"

1/2"
3/4"
1/2"

3/8" R.

2"

5/16"

3/4"

2" 3/8" 3 1/2" 2 3/8"

C 3/8" DIAM.

B

2 3/8"

D

E

1/4"

1 1/2"

45°

1 1/4"

3/4"

3/4"

RADIUS

45°

1/8"

A

8 1/4"

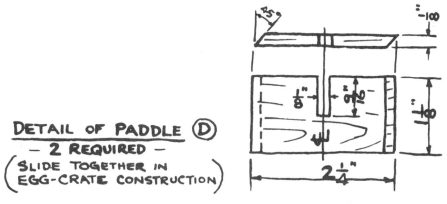

DETAIL OF PADDLE D
– 2 REQUIRED –
(SLIDE TOGETHER IN
EGG-CRATE CONSTRUCTION)

45°

3/16"

1/8" 9/16"

1/8"

2 1/4"

Sailboat

To an imaginative child, a small pond may be an ocean. And a sailboat is the very thing that is needed to make use of it.

A simple sailboat is built with a flat board pointed at the bow end and with a vertical dowel for a mast. A crude sail can be made from a piece of cardboard with two holes by warping the cardboard and pushing it down over the mast. Such a boat can run straight with the wind.

A more detailed boat can have a centerboard, a cabin, a triangular cloth sail with a movable spar, and some rigging.

An elaborate boat can have in addition a streamlined hull, a weighted centerboard, a jib sail, a rudder, detailed rigging and finishing.

No matter how elaborate, any of these boats may be difficult to sail effectively, since, of course, there is no sailor aboard to make the corrections needed to navigate. This doesn't seem to bother a child with imagination, however.

MATERIALS

1 (A) HULL, white pine $3/4''$ x $2\,5/8''$ x $8''$
1 (B) CABIN, white pine $3/8''$ x $1\,3/8''$ x $2\,1/2''$
1 (C) CENTERBOARD, white pine $1/8''$ x $1\,1/8''$ x $2\,1/2''$
1 (D) MAST, birch dowel $1/4''$ diam. x $7''$ long
1 (E) SPAR, birch dowel $1/4''$ diam. x $4\,1/4''$ long
2 (F) PEGS, birch dowels $1/8''$ diam. x $5/8''$ long
1 (G) SCREW EYE, plated; fit over $1/4''$ dowel
1 (H) SAIL, colorful cotton cloth $6''$ x $9''$
1 (I) STRING, cotton 1/16'' diam. x $8''$ long
  (J) GLUE, *waterproof*

Cut out hull from $3/4''$-thick white pine; shape the bow and stern. Cut the cabin from $3/8''$-thick white pine; drill $1/4''$ hole for mast. Cut the groove for the centerboard (keel), and drill holes for pegs at the bow and stern. Cut out the centerboard, mast, spar, and pegs, and attach these items to the hull, using waterproof glue. The spar for the mainsail is made movable by use of a screw eye, and a slot in the end of the spar holds the cord.

Cotton cloth for the mainsail may be white, a solid color, striped, or even a small-flowered pattern. If printed, the cloth should be printed on both sides, as both are visible. The cloth sail is cut out, hemmed, and sewed to fit snugly around the mast and spar. A jib (front) sail and/or a rudder may be added to make it more realistic. Install ropes (strings) of sufficient length to hold the sails at any desired angle.

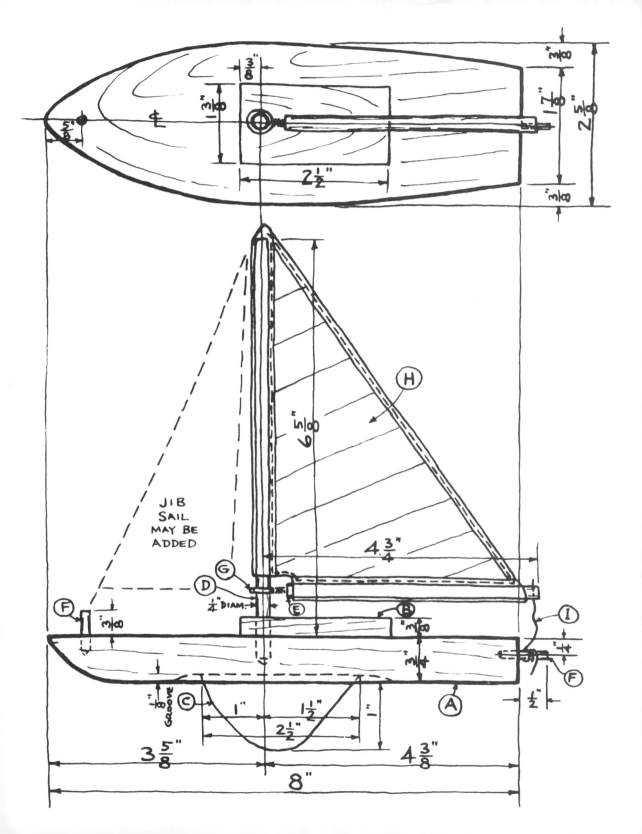

Parachute

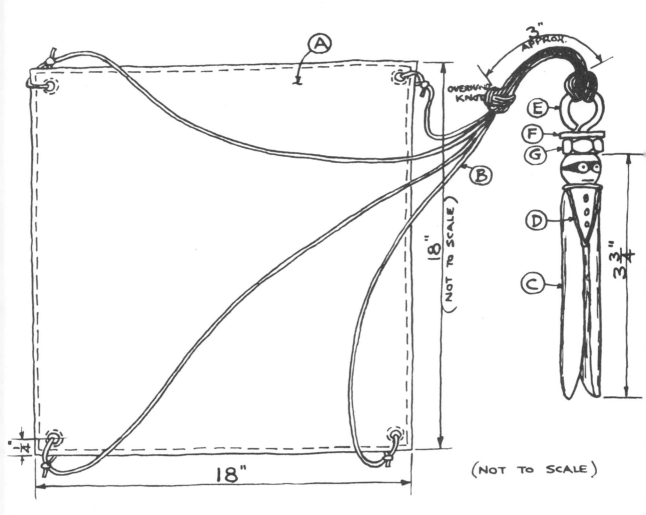

(NOT TO SCALE)

In the early days of the balloon and the airplane, parachute jumps were a spectacular attraction at barnstorming air shows. Children would re-create these descents by making their own toy parachutes. A handkerchief or any other square of cloth can be used. Four cords are tied to the corners and terminated in a knot around the parachute jumper, which is a small stone or a piece of wood of suitable weight. The parachute is packed by wrapping the cords, starting with the weighted end and continuing until all the fabric is wrapped. The entire package is hurled as high as possible into the air. As it starts to descend, the weight causes the parachute to unwrap and inflate in umbrella fashion. Then it will slowly float back to the ground.

MATERIALS

1 (A) CHUTE, bleached muslin cloth 18" x 18"
2 (B) LINES, cotton strings 36" long
1 (C) AVIATOR, wooden clothespin, round type
1 (D) COPPER WIRE, #14 ga. x 10" long
1 (E) SCREW EYE, plated steel, 5/8" outside
     diam., for wood
1 (F) WASHER, flat plated steel 1/4"
1 (G) NUT, plated steel machine nut, 5/16"
  (H) THREAD, colored
  (I) PEN, small felt tip, black

Cut the muslin cloth to the 18"-square size; sew a very small hem around it using colored thread. Cut a small hole in each of the four corners, and reinforce the holes with thread.

The parachutist is made from a round wooden clothespin. He is decorated with a pen, drawing in a face, flying goggles, coat buttons, and so on. Copper wire is wrapped around his body to simulate a parachute harness, but it is also used to add weight. More weight is added with a nut, washer and screw eye fastened into a drilled hole.

To avoid excessive knots, each of the strings makes two of the four parachute lines, being doubled through the screw eye. Tie each line to one of the four corners, making sure the lengths of the four lines are equal. Tie an overhand knot in the bundle of four lines, about 3" above the man.

Pack chute as follows:

Start with the man (parachutist). Grasp the lines as a bundle and wrap them around the man. In effect, he is rolled up inside the lines. Continue wrapping until all the lines and the cloth are wrapped around the man.

Launch chute as follows:

Just throw the bundle as high into the air as you can. At the height of the throw, the weighted man should unroll and drop out, open the chute, and float gently to the ground.

After testing, it may be found necessary to add more weight to the man or to tie the overhand knot at a different point for best action.

For a simplified version of the parachute, the strings may be tied around the corners of the cloth (not through them), and a stone of suitable weight may be used for the man.

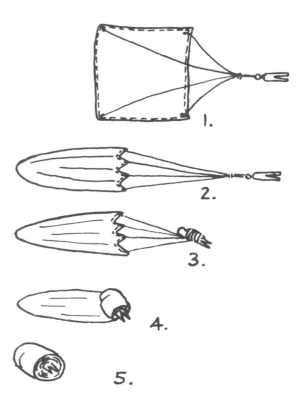

PACKING THE CHUTE

Flying Machine

This helicopterlike toy was known before the invention of powered aircraft. It is a lightweight, carved wooden propeller fastened to the top of a round wooden dowel about the size of a pencil. Place the dowel between the palms of your hands, and rub your hands together briskly. The propeller will rotate rapidly and rise into the air. As it slows down, it will gradually descend to the ground.

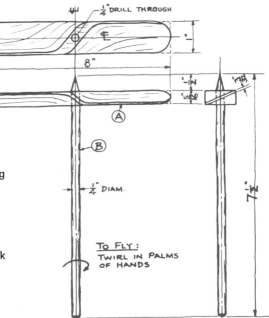

MATERIALS

1 (A) PROPELLER, white pine 5/16″ x 1″ x 8″
1 (B) SHAFT, birch dowel ¼″ diam. x 7½″ long
   (C) GLUE, white

Cut the propeller blank to size, marking the exact center point for the shaft. Drill the hole through for the shaft, being careful to make the hole exactly perpendicular to the propeller. Mark guidelines in pencil for carving the propeller. Carve the propeller, doing a little at a time on each side and each end. Round the ends of the propeller, and smooth it with sandpaper.

Cut the shaft to length from a dowel and sharpen one end in a pencil sharpener. Insert and glue the shaft into the propeller. Test the assembly for balance by rolling the shaft along a tabletop with the propeller turning over the edge of the table. Carve more wood from the heavy end or side until the assembly is in static balance and will roll smoothly along the edge of the table.

The flying machine is now ready to test.

NOTE: NOT TO SCALE

Spool Knitter

This device is only a wooden spool with five nails, tacks or staples driven into one end of the spool. By a knitting technique, a strand of yarn can be passed repeatedly around the nails to weave a continuous tubular rope, which emerges from the hole through the spool. The rope is called horse reins, probably because it was used for that purpose at one time. Horse reins can be used to make belts, rugs, and other items.

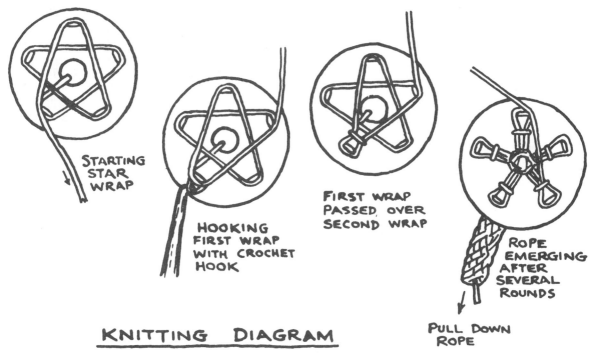

STARTING STAR WRAP

HOOKING FIRST WRAP WITH CROCHET HOOK

FIRST WRAP PASSED OVER SECOND WRAP

ROPE EMERGING AFTER SEVERAL ROUNDS

PULL DOWN ROPE

KNITTING DIAGRAM

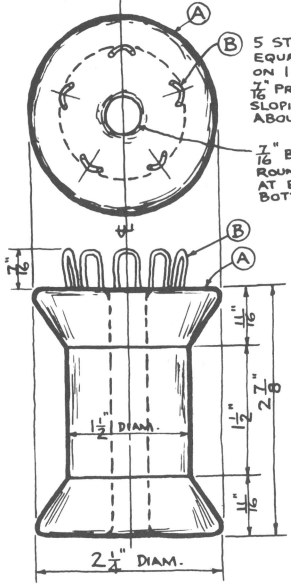

(A)

(B) 5 STAPLES
EQUALLY SPACED (72°)
ON 1⅜" CIRCLE,
7⁄16" PROJECTION, AND
SLOPING OUTWARD
ABOUT 15°

7⁄16" BORE THROUGH,
ROUND OVER EDGES
AT BOTH TOP AND
BOTTOM

(B)
(A)

7⁄16"

11⁄16"

1½" DIAM.

2⅞"

1½"

7⁄16"

2¼" DIAM.

MATERIALS

1 (A) SPOOL, wood 2¼" diam. x 2⅞" long
5 (B) STAPLES, galvanized steel, ⅝" long
  (C) YARN
1 (D) CROCHET HOOK

A large commercial wooden thread spool may be used to make the spool knitter. These are becoming more difficult to obtain, however, so the spool shown is to be hand-turned on a lathe. Bore out the center hole and round the entry and exit ends of the bore, smoothing them so that they will not catch the yarn as it passes through.

Firmly hammer in five staples equally spaced around the top of the spool, canting them slightly outward to help retain the yarn loops. Some prefer carpet tacks instead of staples because the yarn cannot slip off the heads. However, knitting the stitches is a little more difficult with tacks. The knitting is done around the top of the spool, and the finished tubing passes through the spool and out the hole at the bottom.

To use the knitter, run the loose end of a ball of yarn down through the spool until several inches emerge from the bottom. Starting at the top, run the yarn back and forth around every other staple in a counterclockwise direction to form a starlike shape. When the star is complete and you are back to the starting point, start knitting the stitches. This consists of passing the original strand up and over the new strand, from outside the staple to the inside. Carry the yarn to the second staple, wrap it, and again pass the original strand up and over the new strand from outside the staple to the inside. Keep working around the spool, but every few stitches give a little pull on the yarn rope, or horse reins, emerging from the bottom of the spool.

INDEX